An Approach to the

METAPHYSICS OF PLATO

An Approach to the METAPHYSICS OF PLATO *through the Parmenides*

WILLIAM F. LYNCH, S.J.

GEORGETOWN UNIVERSITY PRESS
1959

For information, write: University Publishers Incorporated,
59 East 54th Street, New York 22, N. Y.

Library of Congress Catalog Card Number: 59-7530.

Manufactured in the United States of America
by the Quinn & Boden Company, Inc., Rahway, N. J.

To My Parents

PREFACE

It may be important to say that I did not begin with the title *An Approach to the Metaphysics of Plato through the* Parmenides, but ended with it when this book was concluded. Nor did I begin with any intention or hope of writing a limited summary of the metaphysics of Plato. My one intention, much as a small boy faced with a gigantic puzzle, was to take up the fascinating challenge of this difficult dialogue — the *Parmenides* — and to try different hypothetical solutions as answers to its meaning until all the pieces should fall together into a consistent explanation. Only midway in this task did I begin to realize that the different pieces were discussions of dozens of critical problems in Platonic philosophy, that the whole dialogue could therefore be taken as a kind of textbook summary of Plato's metaphysics, presented in a comprehensive and ordered way, unlike any other of the dialogues.

If the writing had gone otherwise, if it had not been purely exploratory, with no other intention than to be a commentary on a single dialogue, I should myself have very much mistrusted the right or the sense of arriving at this happy result. For I am not the only one to mistrust books generalizing on the metaphysics, or total system, of Plato. It is difficult enough to write a satisfactory study of the metaphysics of Aristotle or of a number of other philosophers who have at least made the task possible by their kinds of thinking and writing. But with Plato we have always taken for granted that the task is even more difficult and subject to vagueness; that his "metaphysics" is spread everywhere in his work, and concentrated nowhere; that it is a spirit and a methodology rather than a thoroughly ordered corpus of the intelligence.

In the face of this tradition it would be folly to enter any exaggerated claim for the *Parmenides*. Nevertheless I do wish to take the larger part of the risk, to claim that he who reads the dialogue rightly has in his hands a summary of the larger part of Platonism. This summary is not achieved without a certain amount of "analysis," and it will always be a delicate question where "the text" (in the most human sense of that word) ends and analysis in any pejorative sense begins. The question is perennial in scholarship. Here I should like to steal the sentence with which Robert S. Brumbaugh concludes the introduction to his *Plato's Mathematical Imagination:* "The choice is between this analytical interpretation and no interpretation worth mentioning."

According to the interpretation of the following pages, Plato in the *Parmenides* is giving a skeletonized and ordered summary of his views on the essence of the Idea Doctrine, on the basic structure of sensibles and numbers, on the nature of unity, the indeterminate, the relation of the contraries, time, the unmeasurable "instant" in time, motion, the Other, the different forms of non-being, his theory of communication, of participation, the nature of identity, the nature of difference, the possibility and source of predication, the way of opinion versus scientific knowledge, the character of limit and the unlimited, the nature of articulation in any unity, the discrete and the continuous, the possibility of real unity in any one-many, the logic of change and transition, of otherness, of relation. Nor are these pieces thrown at us helter-skelter, though some of them are treated indirectly. There *are* great unifying, ordering, and "enabling" concepts, and I have paid special attention to two of them. They are: (1) Plato's theory of participation (it is not easy, in the light of this dialogue, to see how Aristotle could ever have regarded it as a passing, ineffective metaphor); and (2) his constant and complicated success in mediating the original Parmenidean dichotomy between being and non-being.

One could say many more things about the content of the *Parmenides* — but this is only a preface.

In a special way I wish to thank Whitney J. Oates, Chairman, Department of Classics at Princeton University, for his unfailing encouragement. It was in his seminar in Platonism at Princeton that the work was begun. Another special debt is owed to Harold Cherniss, our distinguished Platonist, who read the chapters as they were completed. He was a wonderful example of one who can help without having to agree. Other generous readers were Alexander Koyré, the Sorbonne; Roman Jakobson, Harvard University; W. Norris Clarke, S.J. and Quentin Lauer, S.J. of Fordham University; and James I. Conway, S.J., Loyola College, Shrub Oak, New York. Finally, one can never be grateful enough to editors for their patience and care; in this case I am very much in debt to Mrs. Ruth Bellamy and to Miss Jane Truslow.

For whatever is good in this book I thank many teachers in my past life. Whatever is bad is all mine and will do no harm; it will quickly come to the light under the lamps of all those who know more than I of the metaphysics of Plato.

WILLIAM F. LYNCH, S.J.

CONTENTS

An Approach to the

METAPHYSICS OF PLATO

1

INTRODUCTION

Pre-Notes:

There are five main schools in the interpretation of the *Parmenides:* the anti-Eleatic, the Neoplatonic, the Hegelian, the logical, the metaphysical. This present commentary is completely positive and metaphysical. It views the dialogue as universalizing and rationalizing the problem of contrariety for every level of being. It believes that, while Plato is correcting the Eleatic logic, there is much reason in his using Parmenides as his own mouthpiece.

1

One should almost begin with an apology for writing another commentary on the *Parmenides*. It is a brash thing to add one's own thoughts on the subject, or to try to say something new, after the work of Proclus, Damascius, Hegel, Stallbaum, Natorp, Waddell, Taylor, More, Diès, Robin, Cherniss, Hardie, Paci, Wahl, Speiser, Mackay, Robinson, Ritchie, Wundt, Benn, Cornford, and others. If there is nothing new to say, nothing should be said. If there is a pretension to something new, the pretension in itself is enough to provoke skepticism on the part of the student of Greek philosophy and a blush on the part of the writer. There is, then, no choice but to accept the second of these two alternatives and to face the unhappy consequences. All one can say at this juncture is that the confusing disagreement among the major commentaries still cries for some relatively simple resolutions. I hope I have formulated a simpler and less tortuous reading for the dialogue than have many of these numberless predecessors.

Actually, in one sense, it is quite impossible to write a thoroughly new commentary on a work that is the supreme puzzle of ancient philosophy. I think that the following chapters present a unified and perhaps novel reading, but in the final analysis one finds it is a certain eclecticism that has helped to produce the final product. Substantially there can be said to be five major interpretations given to the *Parmenides:*

1. *The anti-Eleatic or anti-rational school:* The subject of the famous eight hypotheses is the Eleatic One. In the first half of the dialogue, Parmenides has demolished the theory of Ideas; in the second half, the dialectic of the eight hypotheses does the same for Eleaticism. Thus Plato is demonstrating that mere logic can prove anything to be both true and false.[1]

2. *The Neoplatonic school:* The subject of the hypotheses is the divine and superessential One, plus the descending series of progressive emanations of being flowing from it.[2]

3. *The Hegelian school:* The *Parmenides* presents us with a general logic of being on which the Hegelian logic can very well support itself.[3]

4. *The logical school:* The second half of the dialogue gives us a first system of pure logic in the sense in which

1. If the following are cited as examples, a great variety of approach and interpretation among them must be acknowledged: Alfred Edward Taylor, *The* Parmenides *of Plato* (Oxford: 1940), see Introduction *passim* (hereafter briefly cited as Taylor, *Parmenides*); Paul Elmer More, *Platonism* (Princeton: 1926), pp. 257 ff.; Harold Cherniss, "Parmenides and the *Parmenides* of Plato," *American Journal of Philology,* LIII (1932), 122-38; R. Scoon, "Plato's *Parmenides,*" *Mind,* LI (1942), 115-33.

2. For brief summaries of the Neoplatonic interpretation of the *Parmenides,* see Francis Macdonald Cornford, *Plato and Parmenides* (London: 1939), pp. 131 ff. (hereafter briefly cited as Cornford, *Parmenides*); William Francis Ross Hardie, *A Study in Plato* (Oxford: 1936), pp. 112 ff.; Taylor, *Parmenides,* App. E, pp. 145-59.

3. Hegelianism enters into the reading of scholars such as Élie Halévy, *La Théorie platonicienne des sciences* (Paris: 1896), chap. V, and Jean André Wahl, *Étude sur le Parménide de Platon* (Paris: 1926).

Kant gives us such with his categories of the human mind, or Aristotle with his formal logic.[4]

5. *The metaphysical school:* Thus I would generally denominate the elaborate and careful work of Cornford,[5] who would have it that all the hypotheses, save the first (which for him is anti-Eleatic), present us with a positive philosophical, but non-theological, system. He is equally firm in rejecting the negative views of the anti-Eleatic school and the ambitious theological reading of the Neoplatonists. With certain important exceptions, he would hold that the dialogue presents us with a body of serious philosophical theory. Here he is perfectly correct, and my own understanding of the *Parmenides* is indeed positive and metaphysical; but I would summarize my differences with Cornford under three brief headings: (1) I propose that the totality of the eight hypotheses, no part excepted, is both serious and positive in its meaning, and both these adjectives can be applied, therefore, to the first hypothesis; whereas Cornford is as anti-Eleatic and negative here as the strictest member of this school. (2) Secondly, the general philosophical plan I discover, par-

4. One example of this logical view is that of Gilbert Ryle, "Plato's *Parmenides*," *Mind*, XLVIII (1939), 129-51, 302-25. Cf. especially p. 316: "But his questions and his arguments in this dialogue should be classified by us as belonging to the same sphere to which belong, for example, Aristotle's theory of categories, Kant's separation of formal from non-formal concepts, Russell's theory of types and Wittgenstein's and Carnap's theories of logical syntax."

5. Cornford gives us a summary of schools of interpretation at the beginning of his work (*op. cit.*, v-x); similar summaries will be found in E. J. De Vries, *Spel bij Plato* (Amsterdam: 1949), pp. 146-52, and Hardie, *op. cit.*, pp. 102 ff. For an older summary of modern views, see also G. Stallbaum, *Platonis Parmenides cum quattuor libris prolegomenorum et commentario perpetuo* (Leipzig: 1841).

ticularly in the hypotheses, differs substantially from his own. (3) Finally, I tend to see even more logical, physical, and metaphysical questions being discussed by Plato under the deceptive guise of dialectical machinery than he.

I must confess that every one of these readings has been the source of some illumination for me. There will be no commentary in the future that will not be solidly indebted to the careful analysis of Cornford, who has not hesitated to tackle the subtleties of the dialogue line by line. Even the modern Neoplatonists, with whom I thoroughly disagree, can throw considerable light on the dialogue's ultimately fairly simple meaning. As I shall propose, the description they find in Hypothesis I of a pure, indivisible One, unrelated to anything but itself, is perfectly accurate; it is they, therefore, who are nearer the truth about this section than anybody else. The only flaw in their work was not having seen that this whole description could be as validly applied to *anything* that is one as to their hypothesis of a divine One. Somewhat the same could be said for Hegel and the Hegelians. Their penetration helps to illuminate much of the dialectic of Plato in the *Parmenides*, but finding a substantial identity between the two total systems is another matter. There is also considerable truth, though always partial, in the anti-Eleatic reading, but we shall see it is still truer that Plato has written a defense rather than an indictment of Parmenides. And so it goes. One can be grateful to all and still remain critical.

I shall set down here, as briefly and as simply as I can, the major principles that govern the writing of this book:

1. In a search for meaning, one should follow, as literally as possible, the clues presented by Plato himself.

Let me cite a single example: the heart of the first half of the *Parmenides* constitutes an attack by the founder of Eleaticism on the doctrine of Ideas; he sees the difficulties caused by the latter as serious and substantial. The eight hypotheses that follow supply both the logical training and a good many of the actual answers necessary for the solution of these difficulties. One evidential source for this conclusion is simple. At the close of the attack, Parmenides has pointed out to the very young Socrates that he needs a *γυμνασία*, or training,[6] that will be exhaustive and exhausting before he can successfully confront his attackers. *This should be taken with complete literalness as an index to what follows, for it is precisely such a γυμνασία that is given us in the hypotheses.* The precise difference between this kind of training and a pure logic will be made clear in the proper place.

2. For this training *is not* purely logical or formal. It not only supplies some direct answers to the difficulties of the first part; in the range of the actual metaphysical questions with which it deals it sweeps far beyond the narrower range of these difficulties. To such a degree does it do this that it may well be considered a shorthand summary of the whole logic and ontology of Plato. There is no such thing as a pure logic in Platonism,[7] either in the Aristotelian or the

6. 135c, d. (John Burnet's text of the *Parmenides* [*Platonis Opera*, Vol. II] has been used throughout this book. When cited, as here, its title will usually not be repeated.)

7. Richard Robinson, *Plato's Earlier Dialectic* (Ithaca, N. Y.: 1941), pp. 75-76, gives an excellent summary of the objective mood of the Platonic dialectic, though the following may be unnecessarily hard on Aristotle:

Kantian sense. Even the concepts that in the *Sophist* explain the positive and negative judgment (Being, Same, Other), and that in the *Timaeus* explain the structure of the thinking soul, are primarily ontological in their bearing and are as much a theory of being as they are a theory of logic — so too with the methods of analysis given in the hypotheses. It is true that they are meant to equip the mind with firm habits of distinguishing all the senses in which the One can be many and the Many one. But at the same time they are constructing a unified metaphysical system.

The whole second half of the dialogue takes the form of a "philosophy of unity" in a sense that will be briefly explained below (and more elaborately through the course of this whole book). I can go even further to say that the section is a veritable storehouse of Platonic thought and was the most serious kind of expression of the current stage of Platonic philosophy. So many problems dealing both with logic and the real order are covered that I have indicated their general nature in the synopses that precede each chapter. As a result, I think I can make the following suggestion. It has been taken for granted that to grasp the nature of Platonism it is necessary to read all the dialogues and *synthesize* their

---

"By thus isolating it from the source of its inspiration, Aristotle changed dialectic from the highest intellectual activity to a dubious game of debate. This made prominent the idea that dialectic is a training or exercise, valuable scarcely at all for its own sake, but mostly because it prepares the muscles of the intellect to undertake some other task. This idea is very recessive in Plato, although there is a good deal of talk about mental gymnastics in the *Parmenides*." For my part, I should say that there are few pieces of dialectic in the *Parmenides* that are not communicating a metaphysical doctrine; it is, however, unnecessary to eliminate the fact that the final total metaphysical doctrine of the eight hypotheses is also a "training."

spirit, that it is impossible to suggest any one dialogue that will serve the purposes of such a synthesis. But, if my reading is correct, it is possible to offer the *Parmenides* as precisely the work that will — with limitations, of course — answer such a need.

3. What, then, is the first key to the meaning of the hypotheses, or second half of the *Parmenides?* — for therein lies the essential puzzle.

a) They are nothing less than an analysis of the constitutive elements of anything that is a true *one*, or unity, in any order of being. I say "a" *one*, and immediately this point of translation is significant. We should not constantly read "the" One so that it suggests either the Neoplatonic or Parmenidean One or the Platonic Idea. Rather, the word "one" is meant to deal with unity wherever it is found, whether it be a sensible, a number, a definition, an Idea, the Parmenidean One, the Idea of the Good, or, though anachronistically, the Neoplatonic One. Wherever a true *one* is to be found, the total system of the eight hypotheses is meant to be a formal analysis of such a unity.

b) This interpretation applies to all the hypotheses without exception. One of the principal mistakes of Cornford is his agreement with the majority of commentaries in isolating the first hypothesis as anti-Eleatic or negative before he begins to read positive meanings into the remainder. But this opening hypothesis as well is not only serious and positive in its meanings; it is indeed the very basic section upon which the subsequent total structure depends. Moreover, Cornford's main intent is to show Plato as progressively redeveloping the Pythagorean concept of the universe after that had been dismantled by Parmenides. He proposes that the One of Hypothesis I is equivalent to the Parmenidean One and must therefore be subjected to the same critical assault as the all-embracing and unqualified unity of the Eleatics; in brief, it can neither exist nor be known. Thus we are apparently to suppose that the first hypothesis is an anti-Eleatic introduction, which must first get rid of this ancient monster of metaphysics. According to this view, the world of multiplicity and specificity, of the sensible order, of time and space, is then reconstructed on Pythagorean lines in Hypotheses II and III. Actually there is no such progression and the One of the initial hypothesis is as much a description of a principle resident in sensible reality and Becoming as is that of any other section.

In brief, the arguments against the Ideas in the first half of the dialogue had indicated that the unity of the Idea has been destroyed by its dispersion into many instances or particulars. Every attempt to salvage the situation by calling the Ideas models or concepts, or by suggesting that they are present in things, results in similar dilemmas or ἀπορίαι. The One becomes many, the self-identical becomes separated from itself.[8] Now the main task for Plato is really to stress that this "dilemma" of a one-become-many is not merely native to the relation between the Idea and its many participants or copies; it occurs *wherever* you have any kind of *one*, and occurs within the very *inner* ambit of such a *one*. Such a *one* is always a curious mixture of unity and multiplicity. But this mixture involves the very metaphysical structure of every entity and can be thoroughly rationalized — that is to say, we can locate

8. See pp. 35 ff. for the analyses of the arguments against the Ideas.

all the senses in which a thing is one and is many, all the ways in which, despite dispersion and division, a thing remains one.

Plato, then, must be conceived as saying: before we can solve this problem of the breakdown of the unity of the Idea, we must universalize the problem. The dilemmas that issue from the existence of Ideas and particulars are only one manifestation of a question provoked not only by this relation existing between two different orders of reality but also by the relation between the elements of unity and multiplicity *within* an Idea looked at in itself, *within* a sensible, *within* a number. What we must do, therefore, is to analyze the very nature of any being or any *one*, for the two are convertible. We must formulate *a philosophy of unity for any and every order, as well as for the relation between orders.* And this is precisely what we are given in the eight hypotheses. With this philosophy in hand, we should be able to return to the original difficulties of the first half of the dialogue and formulate adequate explanations for them. And this is one of the senses in which the second half is a "training."

Thus early, for the sake of structural clarity, I am proposing the following as the main propositions of a philosophy (or logic) of unity:

Hypothesis I: Here we study a *one* precisely as one and nothing else. Insofar as anything is one in any order, i.e., insofar as it has a principle of unity in it, this *one,* this principle of unity, is indivisible and without parts. As such it is a self-identity and does not enter into any equation or relationship with any of its parts or predicates, or with anything outside of it. But, though this principle exists, it is, as a pure indivisible, not knowable in the technical Platonic sense of knowledge or ἐπιστήμη.

Hypothesis II: To advance to the point of such knowledge we must see that every *one* is, in actuality, a *Whole*, composed of principles of unity and multiplicity; it is a one and many, a limit and unlimited. Of the principle of unity in any such entity we can still say all we have said of it in Hypothesis I; therefore *the content of the latter remains as a permanent achievement, not as something to be cancelled out* by this second hypothesis. Of the Whole we can predicate a long series of qualities *and* their contraries. This series of contraries is dependent on the fundamental contrariety of oneness and multiplicity and is derived from them as foundation; one set of predicates derives from the oneness of an entity, their contraries from its multiplicity.

Hypothesis II A: There is a point of transition in time between any two contraries — such as being and non-being, motion and rest — that cannot be measured by time and cannot be characterized in terms of either of the two contraries or predicates involved. This we call the "instant" or the "sudden." Thus this section, as all the hypotheses, deals with a special problem or element or moment in the structure or history of a *one;* and it is only by understanding *which* problem is being discussed that we will fathom why the law of predicability is shifting in each hypothesis. For sometimes a hypothesis declares that both of two contrary predicates are applicable to a *one*, sometimes that neither of a given pair is applicable. And all eight sections keep shifting between this kind of affirmation and negation. Actually, there is always a good reason for the καί . . . καί of affirmation or the οὔτε . . . οὔτε of rejection. And the sense of the predicability or non-predicability of contraries changes with the problem involved, as we shall see. For example, non-predicability is the law both in respect to the "instant" of II A and the indeterminate or infinite element of IV, but the reasons behind the two negations are as different as the two phenomena under investigation in those sections.

Hypothesis III: Here begins the analysis of the nature (and structural contribution to the Whole) of the two elements in any entity: one and many, limit and unlimited. The *one* is the dominant principle, source of the unity of a Whole, and contributor to its parts of all the specificity and definiteness they may come to possess. In any entity there is only one *One* and but a single source of predicability. If the Others, or members of the Whole, receive all the predicates of contrariety that the Whole itself has received (in II), it is not that they are, *of themselves,* separate, identifiable units, but rather that they participate in the specificity of the one, i.e., through association with the principle of oneness in a thing.

Hypothesis IV: We analyse the nature of the Others (the many member parts, or unlimited, in any entity). They are, *of themselves,* an infinitely divisible multiplicity, which can be characterized by the specificity and unity of neither of any given pair of contraries.

Hypothesis V: A *one* is itself limited in relation to the rest of the real, i.e., in relation to all other *ones.* This is true because of the presence in it of *otherness* or *difference,* a form of relative non-being that limits a *one* and differentiates it from all others. Thus any *one* is a compound of being and non-being, and this contrariety is the foundation for ascribing to it a whole series of other contraries.

Hypothesis VI: As the preceding hypothesis was a study of the relative non-being of a *one* and of the type of predication that results from such a fusion of being and non-being, so this section is an analysis of what is meant by the absolute non-being of an entity and what follows for it in the way of predication. Once again, but for a different reason, neither of any two contraries can characterize it.

Hypothesis VII: So far, we have been submitting any *one* to a careful metaphysical analysis. Now suppose that the non-philosophical or "doxastic" mind analyzes the structure of a being. Such a mind does not grasp the total unity in an entity, but it attempts to keep hold of all the separate units that compose the Whole. This is impossible because this specificity of parts proceeds from the principle of total unity. We are therefore engaged in a compromising mode of thought, where the oneness of a thing and the specificity of its parts both exist and do not exist. The result is the typical confusion of being and non-being, and of all the other contraries, that is typical of what Plato calls δόξα. This hypothesis, therefore, is a study of δόξα and *its* approach to a *one*.

Hypothesis VIII: Once again suppose that the principle of unity does not exist at all in a *one*, and ask what are the consequences for its parts (i.e., the unlimited). Neither, then, will *these* exist. Thus it follows that the oneness in a thing, its principle of unity, is the source not only of the predicability and specificity of its member parts (III) but also of their very being. In other words, the unlimited makes a contribution to the structure of an entity, but this very contribution is made possible by oneness or unity. It is only the imagination that will conceive the ἄπειρον or unlimited as an altogether separate and previously existing reality that awaits the gift of specificity and form from oneness.

4. From this summary it should be clear how I interpret the meaning of the two central words or concepts in the hypotheses: the *one* and the *others.* They constitute the two elements composing any entity,[9] whether a sensible, a number, a definition, or an Idea. We variously call these elements a *one* and *its* parts, a *one* and *its* many, the limit and unlimited in a thing. This will simplify the meaning of the dialogue and we should reject all other more complicated interpretations of the meaning of the two words.[10] I add only two slight modifications to this understanding: (a) In Hypothesis I the *others* represent not only all the possible interior parts or predicates of a *one,* but also all the other realities that exist outside of it. Thus, a *one* in this section is not only self-identical and unrelated to any part of itself, but also to any reality external to it. (b) In Hypothesis V there is not only an affirmation of difference or otherness between a *one* and its parts, but also between a *one* and any other reality outside of itself.

9. I have indicated later that such an entity includes any one total organism of reality, and therefore may also refer to the total organic collectivity of an Idea with its particulars.

10. For Cornford, the word "one" has a variety of meanings throughout the hypotheses. That this should be so "has been obvious to all commentators, ancient and modern" (*Parmenides*, p. 107). My own reading holds that the meaning of the word does not change in the slightest way, though the resulting philosophy of the "one" has any number of possible applications through different fields of the real. (If I do not always cite the pagination of Cornford, *Parmenides*, it is because its progressive argument is always easily located.)

5. I would also say a few words about the place of Parmenides in the dialogue, but with special reference to his position as principal speaker through its second half. How is it possible that he be used as the mouthpiece in what is proposed as a dialectical and metaphysical instrument for the defense of the theory of Ideas? I think that only a full reading of this commentary will supply an adequate answer to that question. But in brief the answer comes down to this:

The Eleatic logic is more accepted than rejected by Plato. Both Plato and Aristotle hold the venerable figure of Parmenides in the greatest respect and the reason is that he is the first great metaphysician of unity. Here in this dialogue it is the major principles of Eleaticism themselves that are used to solve most of the dilemmas that occur as a result of the fusion of unity and manyness in every Whole. The *one* turns out to be the principle of central importance and, although the philosophy of Parmenides receives substantial corrections in the eight hypotheses, still his One wins more battles than it loses. Of the principle of unity in a being we can (in Hypothesis I) say, with one or two modifications, all that Parmenides says of his One. It is the One that is the source of all specificity of parts in an entity (III), and that is the source of their very being (VIII). It is the One that gives unity to a being (III). It is even the One that makes possible all the realities of the spatial and temporal continua (II). It is precisely the absence of the perception of unity that makes possible the description in Hypothesis VII of the confusion of thought inherent in δόξα.

True, the dialogue does introduce serious modifications into the Eleatic logic. These were necessary and they have been considered at some length. My only point is that so substantial is the Platonic fidelity to the principles of Parmenides and so extensive his adoption of them that, once this is realized, there need be no shock from a Parmenides who appears as the defender of Platonism and who is himself the resolver in the second half of the dialogue of the very antinomies he has created in the first half.[11]

6. Finally, I have taken the position that the *Parmenides* is not at all a fantastic interruption in the smooth flow and progression of the later Platonic dialogues, but is a perfectly normal though difficult member in the series that includes the *Theaetetus*, *Sophist*, *Philebus*, *Politicus*, and *Timaeus*. When rightly understood, the doctrine of the "mysterious" hypotheses is again and again identical with theirs. It summarizes a good deal that has preceded and anticipates a good deal that follows itself in the Platonic corpus. Indeed, it is almost a first principle of criticism to expect always that Plato is saying in the *Parmenides* what he has said or will be saying in other parts of his total work. For example, in my reading I have not hesitated to refer certain findings of the *Parmenides* to the passages in the *Republic* and *Phaedrus* on the purity and self-identity of the Ideas, to those in the *Sophist* on the communication between them, to the relating of limit and unlimited as structural members of all wholes in the *Philebus*, to some of the conclusions on the problem of knowledge arrived at in the *Theaetetus*, and, again, in the *Sophist*,

11. There is no need to deal here with the actual influence of Eleatic contemporaries on Plato. The evidence is tersely summarized by Hardie (*op. cit.*, pp. 80-81). Auguste Diès briefly describes the situation: "sur les Mégariques, la critique moderne a plus d'hypothèses que de textes." See *Platon, Oeuvres Complètes*, VIII, 1, *Parménide* (Paris: 1950), pp. 19-20.

to the fully developed Platonic theory of otherness or relative non-being.[12]

As a last word, I can only repeat that in its development of Platonic thought the *Parmenides* is so normal and so representative of the great philosopher's metaphysical doctrine that — more than any other of the dialogues — it might well serve the student as a working outline of the whole. Indeed,

12. If there is any conviction that could be selected as the heart of this study, it is precisely this, that there is a positive effort on the part of every hypothesis to build up all the wide-ranging elements of a total metaphysics of all unity and all being. On the other hand, it is the failure to see this positive and *universal* quality in the eight hypotheses that seems to me to vitiate so many commentaries. For example, there is a precious but little known essay on the *Parmenides* by Merle G. Walker, "The One and the Many in Plato's *Parmenides*," *Philosophical Review*, XLVII (1938), 488-516. It is by far one of the most satisfying essays that has been done on the dialogue. We have both independently concluded that the *Parmenides* is an analysis of elements that must apply to all fields of the real. Thereafter, Mrs. Walker clouds the issue somewhat by calling the term *one* the *Idea* of One and the term *Others* the *Idea* of multiplicity. She then lapses back into considering the hypotheses as what might be called a parallel mixture of the metaphysical and the anti-Eleatic; where you have the *one* in association with the many, you reach a successful *καί . . . καί* predication of contraries that makes being and knowledge possible; where they are disassociated, you have an annihilating *οὔτε . . . οὔτε* predication. Contrarily, I see Plato as using even the negation of contraries as a positive description of some element in being, so that the type of predication involved, whether negative or affirmative, is always a definition. And the sum total of all the types of predication in all the hypotheses is the definition of a *one.* As a result we differ on the meaning of Hypotheses I and IV (which are separate definitions of oneness and multiplicity); I cannot accept her explanation of Hypothesis V; and she has not attempted a clarification of VII and II A. Indeed, as we shall see, the problem of II A is one of the great stumbling blocks to every *καί . . . καί, οὔτε . . . οὔτε* reading of the dialogue. The essence of the stumbling block is that this section is couched in the form of a negation of all predicates and contraries, yet is admittedly describing the positive reality of the moment of transition that makes all motion and change possible. It is certainly not using negative predication to reveal the impossible existence of something.

it was with this possibility in mind that I prepared the brief summaries that precede the chapters dealing with the famous eight hypotheses. Each summary lists the specific philosophic questions raised by each hypothesis; together they will form a convenient index that may somewhat guide the student toward *organization* in his contact with the broad genius of Plato.

2

A DRAMATIC PREPARATION

The Drama:

The Socratic and dramatic form of the Platonic dialogues is analyzed. Despite its formidable exterior the *Parmenides* is also quite dramatic in its structure. The dilemmas of Zeno generate a first formulation of the theory of Ideas by Socrates. Parmenides attacks this theory and forces upon it an elaborating and maturing process. Thus the stage is set for the famous eight hypotheses as a crucial part of this late Platonic process.

2

I believe that the best way of understanding the structural character of the *Parmenides* is to associate it, much more firmly than we have been in the habit of doing, with the characteristically dramatic form of the Platonic dialogues. It has too often been taken for granted that this particular composition has abandoned all such Platonic qualities. That is not so. From beginning to end the dialogue is carefully composed, knows what end it wishes to reach, and plots every step so that this goal must be reached. Such "plotting" is of the essence of the dramatic and dialogue form.

The Socratic and Dramatic Form

Actually, though, it is not meant that this process, either in the *Parmenides* or anywhere else, is artificial, or that the dialogue proposes a goal and only uses those preliminary pieces that will call for the discussion Plato wishes finally to enter upon. The original process is quite the reverse. The nature of the Socratic compositional method is to reconstruct the natural dialectic of the human mind working on the solution of a problem. It begins with a question or a problem or a dilemma, proposes various hypothetical solutions, rejects each as it fails for some reason or other, and finally mounts with the help of such rejections[1] to an answer. If in the final work of composition there is clear evidence of a guiding hand behind the scenes and of a manipulating of the end to be arrived at, that is only because the writer is now in a position to reconstruct scientifically and with remembering deliberation the whole process of search. He can then very well start from his solution and reconstruct the steps that made it possible and necessary.

1. For some of the more striking passages in the dialogues on the use of hypothesis, see the *Meno* 86e ff.; *Phaedo* 92d, 101d; *Republic* 533c, 511a ff.; *Parmenides* 135e ff. The early dialogues are, of course, replete with examples of the ἀναίρεσις τῶν ὑποθέσεων or cancellation of hypotheses. In this connection, however, it is important to point out that there is a constant advance in their dialectical technique. The earlier dialogues contribute considerable space to a propaedeutic on the very explanation of what a definition is, and there are many texts that evidence Plato's difficulty in explaining this (*Meno* 71e-72, *Euthyphro* 5d ff., *Laches* 191e, *Hippias* II 287d ff.; there is an example of the same even as late as *Theaetetus* 146c, d). The respondent tends to confuse a specific example or an enumeration with definition itself (see *Meno* 74d-75a and even *Sophist* 239d-240a). Then again, in so many of the earlier pieces, the first attempts at definition are completely discarded. Passing examples would be the quick rejection in the *Charmides* of ἡσυχιότης and αἰδώς as definitions of σωφροσύνη, or "temperance," or of "a harmony" as a description of the soul in the *Phaedo*. In a dialogue such as the *Lysis*, however, the process followed is the constant refining and modification of an original proposal. But it is not accurate to say that either of these structural developments holds true of the final eight hypotheses of the second half of the *Parmenides*, much as it may be true of the processes of the first part. This warning will be repeated in the proper place. The only real analogy that can be thought of for the eight hypotheses is that which takes place in the divisions and syntheses of the *Politicus* and *Sophist*. There at least, each element that is progressively introduced into the final definition is preserved in its original purity. And so with our final eight divisions. The content and conclusions of each will be preserved in an uncancelled form as parts of a total achievement. (See John Burnet's edition of Plato's works [*Platonis Opera*] for all references to any of the dialogues.)

Thus with the *Parmenides*. In a sense Plato knows exactly what he wishes to accomplish. He wishes to venture upon a thoroughly systematic philosophy (or logic) of all unity (or being). This is the altogether new step achieved by the *Parmenides*. When studying unity or being, he will no longer restrict himself to an analysis of the Ideas; that position will be superseded by a wider one; he wishes to formulate a system that will serve as a common key to the essential structure, not merely of the pure nature of being in the Ideas, but of the inward nature of all *ones*, of all beings, in every order of the real. He does this formally for *being* in the *Sophist*, but he will already have done the same in terms of the problem of the *one* and unity in the *Parmenides*. Both dialogues, however, represent the same search for a universal logic of the real, not merely a search for a more refined theory of Ideas.

The second half, or eight hypotheses, will present us with such a system. The first half constitutes a dramatic reconstruction of the problem and the successive steps toward solution that makes this final system necessary. Thus the total dialogue is all of one piece; it is absurd to suggest a lack of continuity between the two parts. I would even go further by saying that it is unfortunate to use such confusing phrases as the "two halves" of the dialogue. Really, a problem has been set early in the *Parmenides*, various hypotheses are proposed to resolve it, and the eight hypotheses are in their totality, as a unified logical system, the final successful solution to the original problem. In the technical Platonic sense, they form one single, climactic hypothesis.

A skeleton outline of the dramatic movement of the first half of the dialogue might be put thus:

I. Zeno

Zeno is the proposer of a set of antinomies that exist in the sensible order. He finds that, if we accept any kind of principle of multiplicity in being, *then certain oppositions or contrarieties will exist in the same sensible entity;* the like will also be unlike; the one will also be a multiplicity. But this, he says, is absurd.

Now two special qualities of the Zenonian difficulties must be carefully noted and distinguished: (1) His dilemmas restrict themselves to the sensible order, and Socrates will be of the opinion, up to the very end of *his* answers, that if we restrict ourselves to the empirical, no solution for these classical difficulties will be found; (2) The crux of Zeno's argument is that the same one thing does actually but cannot logically contain certain contraries, for then the like would be unlike, the one many. Now the irony of the dialogue is that, for a long period of the discussion, Socrates is in entire agreement with this position, and every one of his early efforts at solution is in the direction of avoiding this dilemma. But every such attempt, taking shape under the various forms of the theory of Ideas, is going to result in the same impasse of contrariety. Socrates suggests that the contrary qualities in the same sensible fact are really different participations in different, mutually exclusive Ideas; the Idea of likeness is not that of unlikeness; the Idea of one is not that of multiplicity. Well and good, but the upshot of the Parmenidean criticism of the Ideas that then follows is to indicate that even on such assumptions everything again terminates in the original dilemma: the Idea, principle of absolute oneness, becomes dispersed and divided from itself; thus the one becomes many and, by implication, the like becomes unlike itself. What else does all this amount to but a recrudescence of Zeno's own problem, albeit on the higher level of the Ideas: there is contrariety in the *same* thing!

I point out this ironic quality of the first Socratic failures this early in order to make it clear that, in a sense, the logic of the *Parmenides* will be forced to return at least partially to the original ground of Zeno and try courageously to face a possibility that it consistently rejects until the very beginning of its second half (i.e., until the eight hypotheses). It is a good beginning to say that the contrarieties of the sensible order cannot be solved by remaining within that order and that we must have a theory of Ideas. But the logic of things will finally force us to acknowledge that even in the Ideas, indeed in the whole range of being, what is one is itself many, what is like is itself unlike. That is to say, it will be seen that contrariety can and must exist within the same entity, whether the latter be a sensible, an Idea, or anything else.

I do not think, therefore, that we really understand either the weakness or the force of Zeno's arguments or the drama of the dialogue unless we see that Zeno turns out to be half right. His partial function is to initiate the great debate by stating the problem of the one-many, the problem of contrariety, in that primitive way in which it strikes the senses of the ordinary man who sees that sensible realities are a curious mélange of ἀπορίαι. The whole first half is the story of the twisting and turning of Socrates in order to escape the confusion of these dilemmas, to keep the *one* a pure one, and the many a pure, isolated many, devoid of all oneness. He makes three attempts to do this: through the theory of Ideas as a theory (1) of participation, (2) of imitation , and (3) of conceptualism. None of these, as stated in the first half of the dialogue, succeeds in maintaining the unity and purity of the Idea. He therefore finally abandons the very effort to preserve these qualities. He is compelled (in the eight hypotheses) to work out an interior logic of all being, according to which any *one* (sensible, Idea, definition, number, etc.) is a mixture of one-many, like-unlike, etc.

Thus, a simple dramatic plan. Zeno is largely right. Contrariety exists within the same field of being, within the same entity. The crude and primitive perception of contrariety is correct.[2] But at the end of the hypotheses, we shall have a system of logic that will have completely *rationalized*, made logical, this kind of "dilemma" of contraries. What was a fact but logically impossible will have become logically pos-

2. The attitude of both Plato and Aristotle is not over-respectful to Zeno, and in this there is a marked difference from their appraisal of the figure of Parmenides. As for the arguments of Zeno, perhaps they are included under the first class in this distinction of Hardie (*A Study in Plato*, pp. 81-82): ". . . there is a reference in the *Philebus* (14c-15c) to the difficulties of the theory. 'Socrates' there distinguishes between different forms of the One-Many problem, some of which are 'childish' and 'popular,' some not. The trivial forms of the problem, he says, are those concerned with the union of many qualities in one individual, and with the unity of a whole which has many parts. The serious forms of the problem arise, not in connection with 'the things that come to be and are destroyed'; but in connection with 'henads' . . . i.e., with intelligible forms." This, indeed, is the traditional way of classifying Zeno's arguments, but it will be clear that I have refused to accept it as the total explanation of their dramatic value in the *Parmenides*. And Socrates himself suspects how the wind will blow.

sible and understandable. The primitive view will have been refined to the point of philosophical intelligibility.

This, I take it, is the dramatic status of the first steps in the dialogue, the argument of Zeno. Let us now examine more closely the successive answers of Socrates, always noting that they are being led scientifically and dramatically to a fresh solution by means of the cancellation of previous hypotheses or tentative explanations.

II. Socrates

A. The Ideas, Proposed as Solution of Contrariety

The doctrine of the Ideas is now proposed by Socrates in such a way as to seem to be an answer to the problem of contrariety raised by Zeno for the sensible world. In other dialogues, the theory has been presented for varying reasons: (1) To solve the ethical problem by inserting into the real order a theory of ethical absolutes that will be able, as against all schools of pure relativism in human action, to provide fixed norms for conduct; or (2) to solve the epistemological problem, so that the fixities of human language and knowledge will have some fixed object; or (3) to solve a purely ontological problem, so that all the phenomena of motion and becoming will have some stable directional points.[3] Here, however, the introduction of the Ideas has as its *immediate* occasion the problem created by the dilemmas of Zeno:

3. In this kind of summary I am greatly indebted to Cherniss' fine article, "The Philosophical Economy of the Theory of Ideas," *American Journal of Philology*, LVII (1936), 445-46.

Socrates feels that only by the separate, self-contained, and self-identical Ideas does he succeed in bringing to pass what cannot occur in the confusing world of Becoming. Only in the world of the Forms can it be shown that a quality or predicate is not its contrary. This seems to him to be the all important necessity of the moment: to discover a region of being where the contraries are, as it were, sorted out with absolute purity, for it is thus that we are presumptuous enough, at this stage, to think that Zeno will be answered. What is more simple to say than that a thing is one by participating in oneness, and many by participating in multiplicity? The two realities that are participated in are completely diverse and thus the irritating question of contrariety seems to be resolved.

About this kind of resolution two things may be said: (1) It is a relatively crude form of the theory of Ideas and tries by a sort of sleight of hand to answer the dilemmas proposed. Even if it were true — which is not altogether the case — that qualities can be isolated in terms of the world of pure being, of the Ideas, this would not quite remove the difficulty that they still co-exist in the form of contrary pairs in sensibles. It would still remain true that, even though there be a region where oneness is not multiplicity, the sensible *one* is also a many. In a word, we would have constructed a world which would have somewhat answered the exigencies of human speech and thought, which *does* isolate a pure self-identity for each quality. But we would not at all have solved the confusing testimony of the sense world, where qualities are still strangely intermingled. The world of language and thought would have been given fairly satisfactory objects, but the world of logic would still have failed to confront the order of the senses. We would still be no better off than we were after concluding a reading of the Poem of Parmenides itself.

(2) I am also going to propose that the theory of participation given so far is early and thoroughly unsatisfactory for the purposes of the present emergency. Before the dialogue is completed, it will be replaced by a much more subtle form of participation — indeed, by a form that is revolutionary to Platonic thought.

The present species of μέθεξις, or participation, limits itself decisively to an analysis of the relationship existing between Ideas and their "particulars." In the second half of the dialogue, a new μέθεξις will be inserted into the Ideas themselves. But it would be even better to say that participation will appear as a phenomenon in the inner structure of all being, not only in that of the transcendent Ideas.[4]

4. This is entirely in line with the general drive of all the later dialogues. For how else are we to explain the preoccupation with the motion of οὐσία and the relative de-emphasizing of the study of the Idea? It is impossible, on the one hand, to agree with the Taylor-Burnet school that the Idea doctrine is simply Socratic and begins to lapse in the later dialogues; or, on the other hand, with H. Jackson that these dialogues are marked by the emergence of a new Idea-doctrine. The truth is broader than that. The preoccupation is with being, but with a being that includes, rather than eliminates, the Ideas. This is true of the *Philebus*, the *Parmenides*, the *Sophist*, and the *Timaeus*. Admittedly, "being" is indefinable (*Sophist* 249 *circa*). Nor is any one attempt to describe it successful. Diès, in his commentary on the *Sophist* (*La Définition de l'être et la nature des idées dans le Sophiste de Platon* [Paris: 1909], pp. 17 ff.) has listed enthusiastic attempts by Zeller, Lutoslawski, and Gomperz to use the definition of being as "power" in that dialogue, but rightly minimizes the notion. What we really begin to find is a series of attempts to list the "categories" in which being is expressed, or the elements of which it is in a sense "composed."

There seems, in general, to be a strong tendency among modern scholars

It is impossible to avoid long-term warnings of what is to occur later in the dialogue; otherwise, notes that are struck earlier will make little or no sense.

Let us look at the present instance. In general, participation means that there is a relation between two types of realities, one of which is a "principle" and source of being, the other a derived and secondary entity that only *shares* in the reality of the first and does not, therefore, in the strict sense *add* to the reality of the first. The first alone truly *is*, the other *has* being. This is, I think, a quite sharp and satisfactory distinction between the orders of Ideas and Becoming.

This kind of thinking will give us some explanation of the nature of the partial, aspiring, approximating being of the sense world. But how will it at all explain away the phenomenon of contrariety in this world? Its first attempt at a solution to all the antinomies of Becoming may be summarized in the following figure:

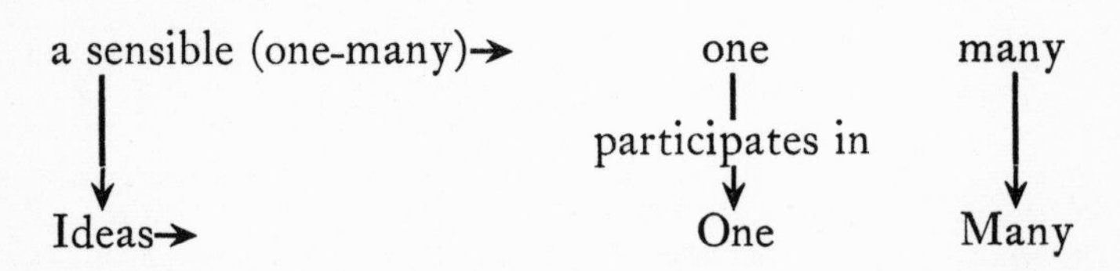

to deny "that Forms-doctrine and metaphysics are co-extensive for Plato"—see Joseph Bright Skemp, *The Theory of Motion in Plato's Later Dialogues* (Cambridge: 1942), p. ix. "Taylor and Cornford differ in so many points that their agreement here is significant" (*ibid.*). There is, perhaps, a little less zeal abroad for identifying God with the Ideas, the soul with the Ideas, or the Idea with the cause of motion. At the same time, I emphasize throughout this commentary that Plato himself is now anxious to construct a metaphysics (or a logic) that will have universal applicability to Ideas, sensibles, numbers, motion, magnitude, time, and anything else that may be included in the "real."

But no manner of isolation of the contraries in the Ideas will answer the difficulty that the same opposites still remain mysteriously bracketed in the one sensible fact (indeed such a community of contraries is never going to be eliminated). Nor will self-identity in the Ideas explain away the fact that the repetition of the Form in many instances produces *some kind* of multiplicity in the Form itself. On the other hand, the final and refined theory of participation in the eight hypotheses can be summarized roughly in the following diagram:

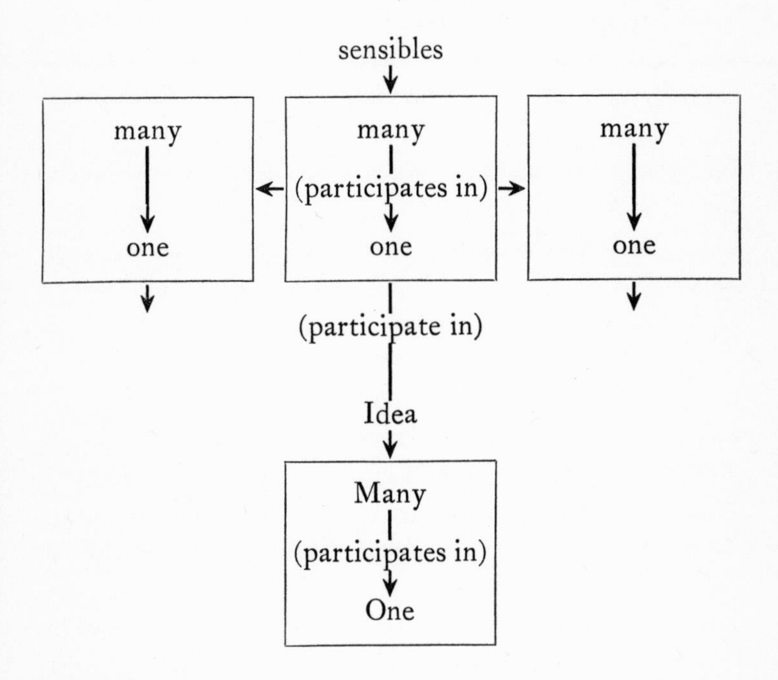

Here we have the expression of a whole series of participations: (1) *Within* the sensible and *within* the Idea, the many elements of any one thing participate in, share, "have" their being from the principle of oneness or unity in any such sensible or Idea. There is only one reality that truly *is* in either sensible or Idea; that is its principle of unity; all its multiple elements *have,* and derive from, this indivisible being. Thus participation becomes a law internal to every level of being. According to this law, the principle of unity in an entity exists absolutely, that of multiplicity receives only a relative being; thus the phenomenon of contrariety is severely modified, for we no longer have two *absolute* contraries opposed to each other. This point is critically important. (2) Thus internally structured (in such a way as will *inwardly* explicate its own problem of contrariety), the sensible also participates *essentially* in the structure of the Idea. It derives its essential structure of contrariety from that of the Idea. (3) Whatever existential form of being the particular has is also derived from the Idea. This actual but participating existence is once again a having and a sharing and does not add to the Idea in any strict sense. (4) Finally, the whole system of Idea-and-all-its-particulars is a One-many that can avoid the impossibilities of contrariety through the same distinction of absolute and relative forms of being. There is never a real duality of principles in any such "organism." It is, then, simply not correct to view the one and the many as *a pair of contrary principles that have equal status* on the same level of being.

Perhaps we may describe the situation that is about to develop in the following way. The early theory of participation was sufficient to explain the relation of absolute-dependent existence between Idea and sensible; it is completely inadequate in the face of the problem of the compossibility of contraries. This would be a matter of essential or structural participation, and we are not yet scientifically equipped to resolve that difficulty. I do not say that there have been no previous hints at such a solution (for example in the *Phaedo*[5]), but the elaborate presentation of a solution in the eight hypotheses is substantially unique and new.

B. The Assault on the Ideas

The method used by Parmenides against this first form of the theory of Ideas is ironic.[6] I interpret the sum of his arguments to mean: You, Socrates, propose to solve the antinomies of the sensible order by creating a world in which there are no antinomies, an order in which the Idea of One is not the Idea of Multiplicity, the Idea of Likeness is not the Idea of Unlikeness. But I will demonstrate that the same antinomies immediately develop in the world of Ideas. When I finish with my arguments, you will not only have the original dilemma on your hands, but it will then exist in a more intense and more universal form. Let us see if your Ideas and your present theory of participation will escape contrariety.

III. The Objections of Parmenides

1. The prime quality of an Idea is that it is "one and the same." The word ἕν is practically synonymous with the Idea.

5. 103c-105b.

6. It is usual for the anti-Eleatic interpretation to see an ironic relation between the attack on the Ideas in the first half of the dialogue and the eight hypotheses in the second half: you use dialectic against the Ideas; dialectic is even more destructive of the Parmenidean One. I wish to stress that the irony I see above has nothing at all to do with this discussion.

And the unity of the form stands over against the multiple presence of the same fact in particulars. But if in any way it enters into particulars and is participated in by them, then it is separated from itself, becoming multiply present in this participating world.[7] Therefore, what is one is in reality many.

2. Somewhat the same thing will occur if we propose that the mode of participation is not that the whole of the Idea descends into each particular, but a part of it into each. For then the result will be, not that these transcendent factors are multiplied but rather, that they are divided. We would be forced to admit the existence of some principle of multiplicity, some possibility of division in them. Thus, whatever the alternatives, whether the things that *become* participate in the whole or in part of the things that really are (i.e., the

7. The natural question arises: what was the original source of these objections against the Ideas? Some would seem to hold that the object of the arguments is the explanation given to Eudoxus of the theory of Ideas: the latter are actually *immanent* in sensibles — cf. H. Cherniss, *Aristotle's Criticism of Plato and the Academy* (Baltimore: 1944), I, App. VII, 536. (This work is cited frequently, and I refer to it hereafter as Cherniss, I.) Cherniss (note p. 538) rejects Philippin's extraordinary supposition referring to the work of Aristotle Περὶ Ἰδεῶν. He indicates (pp. 292-93) that the "third man" arguments against the Ideas were clearly known to Plato "before even Aristotle had come to Athens." Cornford (*Parmenides*, p. 101) rejects a Megarian origin for the criticism of the Ideas in the *Parmenides*. For a view of the completely serious way in which not only Plato but philosophy itself should take the "third man" argument, see Gregory Vlastos' article "The Third Man Argument in the *Parmenides*," *The Philosophical Review*, LXIII, No. 3 (July, 1954), 319-49, and his two postscript discussions in subsequent numbers of the same journal (LXIV, No. 3 [July, 1955], 438-48; LXV, No. 1 [January, 1956], 83-94). Mr. Vlastos is a very skillful analytical philosopher whose respectful criticism of Plato must be confronted. I have not been able to deal with it directly but hope that the total argument I have constructed in this book may have some bearing on the questions he has raised.

Ideas), each of the latter becomes itself in some sense a one-many.

3. Nor is the one-many the only form of contrariety that develops from a theory of participation. We can demonstrate that Greatness becomes small: for if it is a part of the Idea of Greatness that descends into particulars by way of making them large, this part, relative to the whole Idea, becomes smaller. As for sharing in a part of Equality, it is impossible that a part of Equality will make anything equal and not smaller. And so with any hypothetical participation in a part of Smallness. The Idea of Smallness will then be greater than the immanent version of smallness by which it is participated in, and thus, assuming the function of Greatness, the Small will have become Great.

4. Moreover, the very formulation of such entities as Ideas and of their participating relation with particulars immediately creates *ad infinitum* a necessity for finding a factor that itself includes all the reality common to Ideas and particulars (for together they constitute a class!). Thus there is not one Idea of a class, but a second, indeed an infinite number. And we are again in the presence of a multiplied Idea. This is the first appearance in the dialogue of the argument of the "third man."[8]

Here we must pause for a moment to ask what is the true force and weight of these objections, what effect they have on the mind of Plato, and what precisely their dramatic value is in building the structure of the dialogue. In answering such

8. On the uncertain origination of the argument, see Cherniss, I, 293. It is referred to by Plato himself as early as *Republic* 597c, d, and is again mentioned in *Timaeus* 31a, b.

questions, I should say that in all probability they do not strike the mind of Plato as at all overwhelming, that they are by no means the strongest difficulties that could be lodged against the Ideas and that, as a matter of fact, some of them have already been answered in the dialogues. Very likely Plato could have answered them with the logical materials already at hand in his system. But he is keenly aware that, despite their rather primitive quality, these difficulties are intimations, weak though they be, of other and more serious forms of dilemmas and contrarieties that must be faced. He could himself at this juncture have proposed them. Actually he suggests and deals with these more difficult problems when he reaches the second half of the dialogue. Such things as the following must have been in his mind: (a) The science of διαίρεσις, or logical division, had created the difficulty of a one-many in any definition and, correspondingly, in any Idea. Apart from any relation to particulars he is confronted by an antinomy at the heart of the Forms. (b) The nature of number must have become an aggravating difficulty: is any specific number a pure unity or an aggregation of units, or somehow both? (c) At the interior of the sensibles he must have been confronted (the evidence of the eight hypotheses will later confirm this) with antinomical phenomena. The spatial and temporal continua would have suggested a constant contrariety between continuity and discreteness, between oneness and manyness. He therefore allows the present arguments to take their course unanswered; he will in due time add many other less easily manageable antinomies that exist at and in every level of being; in this way he will have forced himself to construct a general logic of a one-that-is-always-many; thus equipped with a more refined instrument he will be able to deal with all the antinomies that seem to proceed from the relation of any *one* to its many, whether the *one* in question be an Idea, a sensible, a number, a definition (enclosing multiple elements in its very inward and essential structure), or a transcendent *one* or Idea (relating itself to a multiple class of particulars). What he needs is a general metaphysics of any one-many able to demonstrate that, no matter what the internal division in a *one*, it remains an absolute indivisible and, no matter what the external dispersion of a *one* in its particulars, it again remains indivisible and unmultiplied. Once again, therefore, I say that Plato allows the present dialectic to take its course; for by its insertion of disunity and dispersion into the Idea it is at least forcing the discussion in a right and necessary direction.

I would compare the progress of events in the *Parmenides* to the past Platonic achievement in still another way. Up to the present moment, Plato has given us a theory of Ideas and of participation that is successful in explaining some of the *existential* differences between Ideas and phenomena. The being of the latter is in some sense derivative and partial and in a constant state of becoming, therefore in a midway region between being and non-being; that of the Idea is absolute and eternal, unchanging, and in some sense "principiating." But this kind of theory in no way touches the structural dependencies and relations between these two forms of being. As a matter of fact it has left a complete and unsettled lacuna between the two in this respect. The sensible is filled with different types of contrariety, the most fundamental forms of which are the pairs of one-many and being-non-being. We must therefore further supplement our thinking on the nature of participation, now in the order of essence and the very inward structure or form of being. We will discover that *in the sensible* there is a participation of a many in a *one*, and that the many, or the element of multiplicity within such an entity, has this second form of *derived* being; thus the fundamental unity of being remains undisturbed even in the sensible and there is no final antinomy here, because only its principle of unity *is,* while its many elements of themselves have nothing but a relative and participating being (though the total sensible *is* a participating being). But all this in turn is true because this kind of metaphysical structure pertains to all being, even to the Ideas. It is not necessary — indeed it is fatal — to keep sensibles mixed with, and the Ideas pure of, contrariety. If we do so there is no solution. It is only by universalizing the problem that we reach an answer.

The sensible, therefore, participates doubly in the Idea, both existentially and structurally. And all the present attempts of Socrates to solve his problem are failures because they restrict themselves to the existential status of the Ideas and do not try to analyze their structure. But the whole dilemma with which we are dealing belongs to the order of essence and structure: how in all logic can contraries exist within the orbit of the same being?

We should observe in the following how Socrates continues to twist and turn in the wrong direction before Parmenides finally begins to lead him through to an analysis of the nature of all being.

Conceptualism

Before the final solution is presented in the second half of the dialogue, two further hypothetical answers are proposed by Socrates by way of avoiding the difficulties inherent in his current Idea doctrine. The first is that of conceptualism;[9] the second is a theory of exemplarism. And, granting any validity to the necessarily double structure of participation that I have just outlined, we shall see how both of these fresh attempts at resolution remain in the identical rut into which the first theory of Ideas has already fallen. Both conceptualism and exemplarism are trying to establish and preserve the absolute unity of an Idea or a *one* that will be able to serve respectively as epistemological and ontological explanations of its class of particulars. In the one case, we feel that there is a real epistemological unity in a class and that is satisfied by the rigorous unity of a purely mental Idea, by *conceptual unity*. In the other case, we feel that there is some kind of ontological unity in a class of particulars and that is taken care of by the equally rigid unity of a transcendental model. Actually, such theories do not even touch on the question at hand, which is the question of contrariety between a *one* and a many in a single common orbit of existence. The

9. One might note these texts as a *locus classicus* for Kantian interpretation of the *Parmenides*. "But although 'Socrates' cannot meet the difficulty about μέθεξις involving the breakup of the indivisible 'Idea,' 'Parmenides' puts him in the right track, as Professor Natorp says, for meeting it, by suggesting . . . that the unity of the 'Idea' comes from, amounts to, the unity of consciousness, the unity which is effected for us when we regard many things from one fixed point of view or ἰδέα" (John Alexander Stewart, *Plato's Doctrine of Ideas* [Oxford: 1909], pp. 77-78).

truth is that the whole current dialectical process is going in the wrong direction and may be described as essentially futile for the present purpose. As a matter of fact, the only real purpose of the two arguments on both concept and exemplar is to show that, granted there are such noetic and ontic facts in being, both can themselves be shown to involve the very problem we are trying to bypass: that of contrariety.

The actual answers given by Parmenides to annul these theories are as follows:

1. *Conceptualism:* If, to save the unity of the Idea, you propose that it is a concept ("for in that case each Idea may still be one, and not experience infinite multiplication"), then you are making the Ideas either thoughts or Thought itself. If they are thoughts, then they have an object that redundantly is the original Idea we have been discussing; and the implication is that we should then have to return to an investigation of all the original dilemmas already discovered in the Ideas. But these amount to a statement of the existence of the contrarieties of a one-many at the heart of these Ideas. Plato dismisses lightly the alternative possibility that the many participate as thoughts in the Idea as Thought.

2. *Exemplarism:* If, on the other hand, they are transcendent models, it is easy, by the argument of the "third man," to indicate the presence of a similar impasse. Between model and instance there must be a common bond of likeness; between model, instance, and bond another common class identity that is itself a model, and so on *ad infinitum.*[10]

10. Plato seems clearly to be referring to and answering this difficulty in the *Sophist* 240a, b. There it is said that the image of a thing is "like" the reality of its model, but Plato does not reverse the relation by saying that the model may be likened to its image.

Thus in every way, no matter how much we twist and turn, the result is the same. I believe again that a good number, if not all, of these arguments are partly verbal and to a degree superficial. Plato himself, in the second half of the dialogue, will indicate more profound and more important ways in which contrariety is rooted in the Idea and in all being. But all these arguments are, at any rate, dramatically valuable because, superficial or not, they have conducted the line of debate back to its original crisis. And it is now becoming clear that a new venture must be made; a more sophisticated theory of Ideas (and of being) must be constructed.

The Final Objection

If the general proposition is correct that what the rest of the dialogue must set itself to is (1) a more resolute concession that contrariety is a fact, and that (2) this fact can only be elucidated by explaining the possibility and reality of contrariety in every field of the real, and therefore in being itself — if this is the case, then the final argument brought by Parmenides is both interesting and confirmatory for our whole analysis.

For what it generally says is that it is impossible for a mind situated in the order of Becoming to know the order of Being, as it is equally impossible that God, situated in the latter order, should know the things of men. The fundamental assumptions of such an argument are that the two levels of reality are essentially different and that, as a consequence, the mind that is related to the one set of entities cannot enter into relationship with the other. Actually, such assumptions correspond perfectly with those latent in the theory of Ideas as it has been expressed up to the present stage of the dialogue. For every effort has been made to keep the Idea pure, one and indivisible, and to keep it untouched by any of the multiplicity and contrariety that are clearly present in the sense order. It makes some sense, therefore, to suggest in this final argument that only a divine intelligence can know such transcendent realities, that the human mind cannot — and vice versa with the order of becoming, that the human mind can know it but the divine cannot.

But it is abhorrent to both the philosophic and the religious instinct to conceive that man cannot know the Ideas, that God cannot know this world. What is more than ever necessary, then, is to pass on to a more subtle study of the fact of participation, such as will reveal a common essential structure pervading every level of the real. If this is so, a mind in possession of such a universal logic as that which we have described many times will be able, at least in the order of essence, to know all the fields of being if he knows any one of them. Up to the present, the separation of these levels has been too radical. We must now adjust the differences, and this is the primary function of the eight hypotheses. These hypotheses we must consider as one total theory, or logic of being. Thus they constitute the fourth, and now successful, effort to solve the problem of contrariety, the first three having been: the Ideas as objects of participation, the Ideas as concepts, the Ideas as models. In the sequence of the eight hypotheses, I must re-emphasize that it is no longer the single department of reality called the Ideas that is being analyzed. It is a broader concept of being, the results of which will have a universal applicability to all that in any fashion *is*.

3

HYPOTHESIS I

The Problems:

If the *Parmenides* is a substantial summary of Platonic metaphysics, this first hypothesis is centrally important. It is completely affirmative and only superficially negative. And it is neither Neoplatonic nor anti-Eleatic.

Anything in any order that is a true *one* contains a principle of complete unity and indivisibility. This principle is also a principle of full positivity that is in a sense above all predication and above all contrariety.

All this is true even of all ones in the spatio-temporal order. Here too there is a sense in which their principles of unity are above all the divisions of space and time.

It is remarkable how much the content of this first hypothesis corresponds to the earlier Platonic descriptions of the Ideas.

3

As a preface to this all-important hypothesis, let us repeat that it is meant by Plato to be eminently positive in character and that the great majority of views conceiving it as anti-Eleatic and negative in force should be rejected. It is, in fact, the key hypothesis among the eight, and its very simple but fundamental conclusions are to serve as the main arch on which will be constructed the elaborate analysis of unity to be given in the remaining seven sections. Admittedly, this first Platonic "essay" on oneness seems to end in a complete impasse, which apparently cancels out the total content of the hypothesis. And this classical problem must be faced squarely by any commentary. But everything up to the moment of the statement of the final ἀπορία must be taken with high seriousness and positivity. It will be sufficient at the right moment to indicate that subsequent parts of the dialogue refer back to these serious conclusions as essential propositions for the movement of their dialectic. And the final impasse itself, which denies the possibility of either being or being known to the *one*, can be resolved in far simpler terms than are traditionally applied to it.

In this hypothesis, we actually begin to study the nature and the structure of oneness, as a *one* of any kind is found in any order of things. We propose to answer the following simple question: as soon as and wherever we have a *one*, what is the first important thing we can say of it? This first "law" of oneness, whatever it is, will be absolutely universal in its applicability; it will hold for the Parmenidean One, for the unity of any Platonic Idea, for any sensible unity, for the unity of any Platonic number, for the oneness of any definition. It will be true of the preeminent Idea of the Good. It would, I believe, be an anachronism to say that these first texts also intended an application to the Neoplatonic One;[1] all that we may say is that the ideal possibility of even such a reference is also present.

I do not enter any claim to the discovery of any *explicit* references to this list of unities. In general, it is better to suppose that Plato himself is satisfied to construct a logic of unity, and I shall leave it to the reader's prudence to orient this logic in various orders of reference. Therefore, if in much that follows I am convinced that Plato is elaborating his theory of Ideas with a greater precision than ever before, he is certainly doing so obliquely. None of the texts deals in a *formal* way with the Ideas, yet again and again they recall the language of that theory. The interpreter must himself take responsibility for the details of his exposition of the manner in which the *Parmenides* is introducing precision into this basic doctrine of Platonism.[2] Yet the capacity for reference seems very clear.

1. Dodds ("The *Parmenides* of Plato and the Origin of the Neoplatonic 'One,'" *Classical Quarterly*, XXII [1928], 129 ff.) has developed the theme that Neoplatonic interpretations of the dialogue go back to the first century, and perhaps further.

2. In general, however, we will be able to use three norms for the

The case is somewhat different with the order of the sensibles or Becoming. There are so many *formal* discussions of sensible phenomena, of body, magnitude, motion, time, age, the discrete, the continuum, that we must ask how and why this can occur if we are being given a universal, representative logic of unity. The reason is clear enough to me, but I wish to present it as a discussable proposition. It is simply that all these phenomena of the space-time world create special problems for the referability of our general logic to them, and they must therefore be treated in an itemized way. Thus, it would be sheer nonsense to suggest that the passages dealing with magnitude, time, the continuum, etc., apply in any way to all other fields of the real. *They must rather be taken as parentheses in the march of a universal dialectic*, so many pauses where the Master of the Academy is asking himself if this dialectic can possibly be true for these special problems. This compositional principle will become clear as we examine the structure of Hypothesis I.

A Brief Summary

Briefly, the whole section tells us that wherever there is a *one* certain basic things may already be said about it. It is,

validity of any series of applications of this universal logic to the Ideas. We will have to ask if such a series has a triple consistency: (1) *Internal:* do the applications coalesce among themselves so as to form one total, consistent theory? (2) *Textual:* do they make sense with, are they conformed to, the theory of Ideas as it is expressed in the total corpus of the dialogue? (3) *Historical:* does any particular application make Plato say what he might plausibly be saying at such a moment in the history of Greek philosophy? As a matter of fact, this triple norm might also be a test for our general logic, before an application is ever made to the Ideas.

in the first place, a pure indivisible without parts, without any structural division of beginning, middle, or end. Already it is difficult to see how such a first logic does not immediately collapse for sensibles, but that question will have to be discussed in its separate place. We are further told that this *one* is not identical with any real or hypothetical part or member of itself. Therefore, all predication is impossible for it. And this is true not only of a Neoplatonic One but of anything that is truly one, even of a sensible. Since it is rigorously a self-identity, we should not even say that it is the same as itself; for, as Aristotle himself points out, even the notion of sameness with self connotes a duality.[3] But the principle of oneness, precisely as oneness, precludes *all* duality. Whether we take all the negations with which Parmenides describes his One or all those with which the Neoplatonists will describe theirs, the really interesting thing to note is that Plato is referring the same series of negations to all unity. One or two of the isolated exceptions that Plato refuses to adopt from the predicates of either Parmenides or the Neoplatonists (granted always the anachronism) are analyzed below.

Thus, in brief, the first hypothesis lays down the two basic laws of non-divisibility and non-predicability for anything that is truly a *one*. Certainly it will be necessary to discover other structural principles and laws existing in a *one*, but these will be the business of subsequent hypotheses and will in no sense cancel the achievement of the first.

3. *Metaphysics* 1018a 7-9.

Hypothesis I

Explanation of Shifting Predication

Another remark may be necessary for guidance through the maze of these eight long arguments. Superficially, the most curious element of the *Parmenides* is the way in which it is constantly making the most varying and contradictory statements about the predicability of the members of contrary pairs of qualities to the concept of a *one*. In the first hypothesis, for example, no member of any contrary pair, whether like-unlike, same-other, equal-unequal, may be ascribed to a *one*. In the second hypothesis, *both* members of any contrary pair are predicated of it. In the appendix to the second (II A), there is a moment in any *one* (that is resident in time) where once again neither of the contraries belongs to it. In Hypothesis III, both of the contraries that in Hypothesis II were shown to mark a *one* are now said to be predicable of any member-part of a *one*. In the fourth hypothesis, where these member parts are studied separately from any association with unity or a *one*, another complete negation of the contraries occurs for these members. Hypothesis V next considers each *one* as a limited concept that is other than any other *one*, and thus it becomes a curious mélange of being and non-being and of many other forms of contrariety.

I have already said that what must be followed in all this is the shifting nature of the *totally different problem* in the *same one* that is being studied in every case. One ought not to decide beforehand that Plato is playing with words and performing anti-rational tricks to show that, if you are clever enough, all things can be demonstrated to be true and not true of the same thing.[4] Historically, what Plato was confronted with was an over-simple understanding of the principle of contradiction. According to this simplification, there is an absolute dichotomy between being and non-being — if a thing is, it can in no sense not be; if it is one of two contraries, it can in no sense be the other. It was therefore necessary to supply a training that would indicate to the mind all the refinements this dichotomy was neglecting. Far from being scandalized at the constant manner in which Plato, through the course of the *Parmenides*, will be shattering this overly incisive dichotomy, we must first learn to ask what principle in a *one*, or what quality in it, or what phenomenon in which it is engaged, is being brought into question. Isolate the problem and you have your hands on the root reason in each case for the rejection or affirmation of *both* contraries, of both being and non-being and all other pairs. For the sake

4. Cf. Taylor, *Parmenides*, pp. 10-11: "We can understand why Plato . . . should counter by saying in effect to his critics: 'Turn the kind of logic you are accustomed to exercise upon me and my Socrates against your own fundamental tenet, and see how you like the result. The contradictions in which you think you have entangled me are nothing to those in which I can involve you by playing your own game with your own doctrine. I can easily do with you as Zeno did with the critics of his master Parmenides — give you back as good as you bring and better, in a way which will be highly diverting to a lover of dialectic.' "

Cf. More, *Platonism*, p. 257: "The interpretation of the *Parmenides* thus depends upon the solution of this crux: we have the whole doctrine of Ideas subjected to a process of destructive logic to which Plato makes no direct answer either here or anywhere else in his writings, and by the side of this we have an unwavering statement of the reality . . . of Ideas. Given this dilemma the only way of escape would seem to be through holding that Ideas do not come to us by a process of metaphysical logic . . . and that the method of reasoning employed against them by Parmenides . . . is all *in vacuo* . . ."

of clarity I should repeat two examples. If you are analyzing a *one* that is engaged in time (II A), there is certainly an "instant" in the motion from one contrary to another to which we can, in all logic, apply neither of these contraries. But if you are discovering that a *one* has a principle of *otherness* isolating it from every other *one*, a new type of predicability intervenes and you can assert *both* being and non-being — plus a host of other contraries — of such an entity.

Here in the first hypothesis the aspect of a *one* that is under examination has already been stated; it will, then, have its own law of predication. We are looking at oneness precisely as such; we are saying obliquely that there must be resident in any thing (that is truly *a* thing) a principle of absolute unity, and to this principle neither of any two contraries can be referred. Thus the hypothesis becomes the first of eight different essays on eight aspects of unity. We are now in a position to examine its basic point in detail.

THE TEXT OF HYPOTHESIS I
(*137c-142a*)

In the order of their appearance, the propositions of the first hypothesis are the following:

Divisibility	A *one* is not many.
	A *one* has no parts.
	A *one* is not a whole.
Articulation	A *one* has neither beginning nor middle nor end.
	A *one* is without limits.

Figure	A *one* is without form, being neither straight nor round.
Place	A *one* is not anywhere, being neither in another nor in itself.
Motion	A *one* is neither in motion nor in rest.
Predication	A *one* is neither the same as another nor the same as itself.
	A *one* is not other than itself nor other than another.
	A *one* is not like itself nor like another.
	A *one* is not unlike itself nor unlike another.
	A *one* is not equal to itself nor to another.
	A *one* is not unequal to itself nor to another.
Time	A *one* is neither of the same age as, nor younger nor older than, itself.
	A *one* is neither of the same age as, nor younger nor older than, another.
	A *one* does not exist in time at all.
	A *one* does not have past, present, or future time, neither was, nor is, nor shall be.
Conclusion	A *one,* therefore, has no share in being; it is not.
	A *one,* therefore, is not even one.

A *one,* then, has neither name, nor definition, nor is there knowledge, sensation, or opinion of it.
But it is impossible that all this be true of a *one.*

I have taken the liberty of dividing these propositions into categories: *divisibility, articulation, figure, place, motion, predication, time.* It is at once possible to detect a strong correspondence with the major negations ascribed to his One by Parmenides. The latter denies that his One Being can be divided; it is a homogeneous continuum, all alike and not divided by difference; in it there can be no coming-to-be or perishing; it is immovable, and therefore cannot be spoken of as in motion; it neither was nor shall be, but simply *is;* therefore it does not course through an age cycle. Such a correspondence has its reasons and should be discussed.

Actually, what is happening is that Plato is adopting the principal negatives of Parmenides, but is communicating a complete universality to them. They hold not only for the Parmenidean One; they are true of all ones, of One taken strictly as such, wherever oneness occurs in any order of being. Since, however, the major problem for understanding the very possibility of unity is to be found in sensibles, the major part of this first Platonic essay on unity revolves around this order of things. Plato is thoroughly aware that the basic ἀπορίαι of Greek philosophy have been created by Parmenides and that the latter, for all his shortcomings, is the metaphysician par excellence among the pre-Socratics. The eight hypotheses can be viewed as a constant analysis of the Eleatic logic, an analysis that sometimes accepts, sometimes rejects, sometimes modifies the formulae of the latter. I am suggesting below that this first hypothesis unhesitatingly applies the substantial conclusions of Parmenides to any *one*. But it does not commit itself so completely as to be unable to proceed much further and to add serious later modifications.[5] For example, the hypothesis does not say with Parmenides that the One is *unique* (μονογενές), i.e., that there can only be one such thoroughgoing One without any duality or predication. Thus it will be possible for Hypothesis V, which treats of the nature of *otherness* as rooted in oneness, to reveal the metaphysical root for the existence of many *ones*. And Hypothesis II will declare that every entity which is truly *an* entity, though it does indeed contain an indivisible principle, is in reality a Whole compounded of unity and multiplicity.

At any rate the first hypothesis, by its careful omission of a single adjective, is saved from any exclusive reference to the Parmenidean One.[6] By the same token, it may be said

5. There are three outstanding differences between the Parmenidean and Platonic propositions: (1) Parmenides says that his One Being is limited, Plato that his is without limit. But the interior logic of the Eleatic school calls for the total exclusion of non-being, and Melissus saw that the One Being of his master must therefore be said to be "without limit." (2) The Parmenidean One is *unique* (μονογενές), that of Plato is not. This difference is analyzed above and under Hypothesis V. (3) Parmenides declares that his Being *is*; the Platonic *one* finally does not even share in present existence. We must delay the discussion of this difficult point until we examine the true meaning of the conclusion of Hypothesis I.

6. I might point out here that even Cornford (*Parmenides*, p. 117) also falsely deduces that the quality of uniqueness (μονογενές) is contained in the present hypothesis of Plato. This is a perfect example of a theory (the supposed anti-Eleatic nature of the hypothesis) being allowed to imply a situation that does not exist.

in passing, there is no mention of the concept of eternity[7] for the *one* that is here discussed, and while the whole section could deal hypothetically with a Neoplatonic One, it is impossible that this be exclusively true. Thus there is no restriction of the potential existential referability of these initial Platonic propositions. They apply to all *ones*.

A Running Summary

If Plato were writing a formal essay on unity as such, he would perhaps have put it somewhat as follows:

Divisibility

Any one thing, precisely as one, precisely as it is, or contains, a principle of oneness, is certainly not that which is its very contrary, namely, multiplicity or manyness.[8] As such it has no parts,[9] for if this principle, too, were to have parts, then we would be forced back *ad infinitum* to discover a principle of unity that would in turn unify these parts. It is, therefore, not a sum of parts, nor can it be inwardly articulated into any structure of beginning, middle, and end which would denote partness.[10] With equal consequence, it is impossible that it be limited,[11] for such a notion would also imply at least a basic division into beginning and end as limits. And

7. This is, of course, an essential quality both for the Neoplatonic One and the Platonic Idea. It is very curious that all mention of it is omitted. It can only be deliberate, in order to leave the frame of reference of the dialogue free of any such explicit existential status.

8. 137c 3-4.

9. 137d 2-4.

10. 137d 4-5.

11. 137d 6-8.

no kind of physical form, whether straightness or roundness, can ever characterize any kind of real unity. All these qualities involve division.[12]

We can pause here to restate the general tenor of the Platonic logic. Obviously the mind will already be disturbed and will ask the question: how possibly can these conclusions apply to the world of multiplicity and change? Though clearly they pertain to any other order of unity we have mentioned. But for Plato, in a sense, the question is irrelevant. He could easily turn the question into the form: are there actually real *ones* in the sense world? If so, then our logic applies to them; for all that we have thus far said of oneness is irrefutable; it has been simply the analysis of the concept of unity. There may be any number of diverse principles in any unified fact, but it must also contain a principle of unity that must be in every way undivided. This is true even of such "ridiculous" entities as hair, mud, dirt.[13]

Furthermore, it would not follow that because a *one* is "spread" over many component parts its indivisibility is destroyed. All purely physical metaphors such as those of the "sail"[14] and the "day"[15] of Part I are totally misleading, and we shall only be safe if we remain within a purely metaphysical analysis of oneness.

Place (138a-b)

It is wrong, too, to ascribe the quality of "being in place" to pure oneness. Place, of its very nature, denotes a relation

12. 137d 9-138a 1.
13. 130c, d.
14. 131c.
15. 131b.

of part-to-part contact between a thing contained and a container that "places" it; but our previous total elimination of partness in oneness makes this quite impossible.[16] And even if we were to suggest that a *one* is at least in *itself*, this by no means reduces the problem. For "to be in self" implies some kind of duality,[17] and this is not present in a *one*.

So far as sensibles are concerned, we are meeting a series of statements throughout this hypothesis that would run to one general effect if applied to the problems of this order: there is a principle of indivisibility even in the realities of the spatio-temporal world; this principle, though present in space and time, cannot properly be specified as spatial or temporal. So far as they are *one*, the very things whose nature is to possess magnitude, figure, place, and successive moments in time must also escape all such predication. Parmenides is partially correct. Everything that is truly one being, insofar as it is one, escapes all differentiation or divisibility, whether this should seem to come from space or time. We may again remember that, according to Hypothesis II A, there will be a Platonically defined moment between any two points of change — let us say from A to B — that cannot be measured by time, that can only be called a timeless interval and that in this sense is not engaged in time. But Hypothesis I is already saying something sharply analagous to this: there is an indivisible in sensibles that cannot be characterized by any of the ordinary measurements of space and time.

16. 138a 3-6.

17. 138a 7-b 5. Aristotle, too, would say (*Physics* 210b 21) that the primary sense of "in" implies a relation and it is impossible for a thing to be in itself.

In the case of the Platonic εἶδος or the Neoplatonic One, there is no problem and no need to show the application of our predication. Our description of a *one* thus far matches the Platonic and the Neoplatonic descriptions perfectly. For both are indivisibles and self-identities.

Motion and Rest (138b-139b)

Because it is fundamentally important to the logic of this hypothesis, let us repeat that any *one*, any principle of indivisible unity, is neither in itself nor in another. This is to limit it, for the time being, to being a principle of absolute and unrelated positivity, which allows for no division whatsoever, even such as would allow us to describe it (in a judgment) as identical with self. For even this purely tautological judgment is liable to misunderstanding and to the intrusion of some confusing concept of duality. In other words, we are being given a more radical, a more absolute first description of oneness than was even accorded to the ontological fixity and immobility of the Ideas. These have traditionally always been described as stable, motionless, always the same in themselves, at rest, not subject to confusion with anything but themselves. When now we insist that a *one* is subject neither to motion nor to rest we are neither constructing a sort of byplay of hopeless antinomies nor are we saying anything that need contradict our basic doctrine of Ideas. I repeat: we are simply being more absolute and are getting down to the first bedrock of reality, to the principle of radical positivity in all things.

Thus it is inconceivable that this principle become, by any

kind of change, anything other than itself, for then it would no longer be one but two.[18] Nor can it suffer any kind of change in place, for this would involve the revelation that a *one* has parts and is capable of a step-by-step transition into another place.[19]

But neither can such a *one* be at rest. For this would reduce it to being "in the same,"[20] and our first rigorous description of oneness precludes even this. It is, therefore, in this sense that the principle of oneness in any object, and in any order of the real, is neither in motion nor at rest.

I do not have complete sympathy with either the Neoplatonic or Hegelian reading of the *Parmenides*, but it is impossible at this stage not to reiterate that each of these systems has its own ray of light to shed on the dialogue. And here it may be pointed out that the critique of the abstract intelligence by Hegel does have some relevance to our present problem. There *are* first fundamental perceptions of factors in reality that have their incomplete truth, that can in some fashion be isolated by the mind, but that must in due time be lifted up into a higher picture of relations before they make complete sense. Hegel himself has proposed a first moment of anything that is a moment of absolute immediacy and that must be transcended through a negation of otherness before it can enter even into such relation with itself as is involved in self-identity.

18. 138c, d, e.
19. 138d.
20. 139a.

Predication (139b-140d)

We now enter upon a new series of negations in which we refuse to identify a *one* with either member of three pairs of contraries: same-other,[21] like-unlike,[22] equal-unequal.[23] And these negations hold whether these contrarieties are studied as possible relations not only between a *one* and itself but also between a *one* and anything other than itself. This section will become clearer if we understand that there is a double universality of range for its conclusions: (1) First of all, the three pairs of contraries have not necessarily been chosen for any purpose special to themselves. They are really symbolic of all possible qualities and their contraries, and theoretically the list could have been stretched to the infinite. (2) Further, the concept of "other" in these passages is also universal. But, in general, its range falls into two broad divisions. It covers any possible member-part of a *one*, where this *one* is a Whole with such members. But besides these interior "others," it may also include any other thing that lies outside of any particular *one* and therefore symbolically represents the remainder of the real. Our present task is to see how it is true of any *one* — whether a pure One (such as the Parmenidean Being or the Idea of the Good or a Neoplatonic One) or a *one* that is a Whole with members (such as a sensible entity, a number or definition) — that it does not, in this first dialectical moment, enter into a relationship with anything, whether with itself or with an "other."

21. 139b 5.
22. 139e 7.
23. 140b 6.

Actually, if we keep these few structural meanings in mind, what is now being said is quite simple and is only a further clarification of what has already been said. Our *one*, a principle of complete indivisibility, is a fact of absolute positivity and self-identity that is not to be equated with anything save itself — and even this self-identity must not be so put as to involve any kind of duality.[24] It is purely itself and does not yet enter into any kind of relationship with anything other than itself, whether the "other" be outside of it or be a member-part of itself. Neither oneness nor any other concept *of itself* bespeaks any relationship. This is true not only ontologically but epistemologically, for we cannot perceive any kind of relation or predication unless there is a first absolute perception of each of the factors involved. Thus we may isolate as a key sentence the following: "It does not belong to a *one* to be other than anything."[25]

One important observation may be added here. It would be possible to explain the present section by indicating that any one factor is not to be identified with any other factor in the universe. And this would be altogether in line with many of the classical Platonic descriptions of the Idea doctrine. But something more than this is being said. The full proposition is not only so much; it also insists that a *one* cannot be identified *with any other predicate or with the contrary of that predicate.* Later (in Hypothesis II) we shall see that a *one* is seen as a whole of parts, which is both the same as and different from the sum of its parts. Thus, on the basis of this equation with and difference from a set of entities

24. 139e.
25. 139c 4-5.

that are itself, we shall have reason to apply a whole series of contraries to a *one*. Now, however, this *one* is being first revealed as a completely indivisible principle, which in this first "moment" does not suffer such division as can be the basis for the inherence of any kind of contrariety in it. Until an entity is seen to be composed of a principle of unity and a sum of parts in the concrete identical with and different from that principle, it is impossible to say that this entity is identical with or different from itself. Nor can any other kind of contrariety be predicated of unity as such. We are again, therefore, in the presence of the interesting fact that much of the description later to be assigned by the Neoplatonists to their One is also true of any *one* in any order of things. For there is a sense in which a *one*, as one, is above all predication and above all contrariety. It is a transcendent principle, indeed. And we are coming to realize that Plato is finding no difficulty in applying either the Parmenidean or the Neoplatonic logic to all oneness. But we note again that he never includes the word μονογενές (unique) as used by Parmenides to restrict his system to only one One; and he never uses the word ἀΐδιος (eternal) to restrict this logic to some kind of mystical, superessential One. We repeat: he never uses any existential adjective that would limit his conclusions to any one existential status for the One; his findings are all in the order of the essential and are, therefore, universal. They extend to the concept of unity as such, in whatever order any kind of unity be found.

Time (*140e–141e*)

We are now in a position to understand in what sense it may be said that a *one* is not in time. For this is the conclusion of the next section of the first hypothesis, which reaches its climax in the statement: "a *one* has no relation to time and is not in time."[26]

The proof for this conclusion is very simple. Time is considered as a successive series of existences for the same thing in past, present, and future. The result of any such series is that a *one* becomes older than itself and is, therefore, also younger than itself. This implies a difference and division between a *one* and itself. But, with equal logic, anything passing through these stages is always the same as itself, and exists for a time equal with itself. But this absolute thing called "oneness" has already been dialectically denied any relationship of difference or sameness, even with itself. Thus it has no place in time and we cannot predicate of it any of the three stages of past, present, or future.

The fascination of such passages for the Neoplatonist is obvious. And it is only a little less difficult to apply them to the Platonic Idea. The real difficulty again occurs in the case of sensibles whose very nature is succession and whose very name is γένεσις, or Becoming through stages of time.

Yet there is no more difficulty, so far as time is concerned, in establishing an absolute oneness in any real thing that remains an unchanging, undivided, absolute, self-identical fact through all succession than there was in the previous demon-

26. 141a 4-5.

stration that a unified spatial magnitude retains some principle of absolute indivisibility, no matter what dispersion in space its parts suffer. There is, therefore, a sense in which oneness, even its instances in space and time, is always above the cruder understanding of location of a thing in both space and time.

For actually we must remember that the more vulgar conception of visible things sees only the dispersion of spatial parts and temporal moments in them. It requires the philosophical mind to penetrate to the fact of oneness and indivisibility under all the more immediate evidences of the double spatio-temporal division. Plato will later devote an entire hypothesis (VII) to an analysis of δόξα, of the non-philosophical habit of mind that cannot penetrate to unity. But now he is preoccupied with the first object of the philosophic spirit, with the oneness that can be discovered even in time succession.

Once you admit any kind of time process into the principle of indivisibility we have been discussing, you are then forced to introduce certain impossibilities into the very concept of a *one*. Let it at all advance in age or time, and it then is, or becomes, both older and younger than itself.[27] But, by the same token, it is always of the same age as itself.[28] Now Plato has already rejected from the ambit of oneness all such notions as inequality (younger, older) and sameness. His ground for rejecting them here[29] again must be the same; they all involve the entrance of some kind of duality or multiplicity

27. 141a 5 ff.
28. 141c.
29. 140e-141a.

into the picture. Once again, then, what he means to say is that even in time a *one* is a principle of absolute positivity, allowing for no division whatsoever.

This, I propose, is the proper place to pause in our analysis of the first steps of the new Platonic logic. The few remaining lines, which now bring the first hypothesis to a close, present an altogether special problem of interpretation and I have chosen to devote a separate chapter to their meaning. They seem on the surface to sweep aside in a few rapid gestures all the positive conclusions at which we have arrived. We shall have to confront that difficulty in a moment.

In the meantime, it may be good to add two notes indicating the relevancy of the logic of the first hypothesis to the theory of Ideas, for we must in no sense understand that this logic is being created as a substitute for that theory. First of all, I should like to indicate that the total early doctrine not only remains intact but has, if anything, been fortified. Secondly, it is important to realize that if the hypothesis does apply in a univocal manner to all the fields of the real, then a disturbing quality arising from the general tone of early Platonism has been removed: if the description of any *one* as it is given here in its first phase can be applied both to the Ideas and the sensibles, then the gap between these two worlds has been considerably diminished, and the world of sense begins to assume a greater intelligibility.

The First Phase of the Ideas

Plato has always held that any Idea is not to be confused with any other Idea; it is uniquely, permanently, and purely itself, and not to be identified with any other reality. All the Ideas are independent, cosmic factors. No later theory of κοινωνία, or communion between essences will disturb this foundation stone of metaphysics. As a matter of fact, the very possibility of communion, logical or ontological, depends on these distinctions.[30] But this kind of thinking is completely supported by the logic of the present hypothesis. Indeed, we must in general remember that the first half of the dialogue has closed with the affirmation by Parmenides of the necessity of Ideas over against any kind of technical argumentation, and therefore the first hypothesis, with its own affirmations, may now serve as the perfect transition to the new dialectic.

Actually, so much of the work of the whole Platonic corpus is briefly summarized by this hypothesis that it is impossible in our compass to do justice to the topic. The Platonic vocabulary is replete with words and phrases that indicate the metaphysical intention we are discussing. Each Idea is αὐτὸ τὸ εἶδος, αὐτὸ καθ' αὑτό; it is the kind "set off, disentangled from its fellows and seen in its full purity."[31] It is ἄμεικτον,[32] unmixed with any other essence, and μονοειδές.[33] Each form is an ἕκαστον, an *each*, separated from all. Even such terms as καθαρός and εἰλικρινής indicate not only the Idea transcendent but the Idea pure and undiluted by the presence of any other cosmic fac-

30. Cf. Raphael Demos, "The One and the Many in Plato," in *Philosophical Essays for Alfred North Whitehead* (London: 1936), pp. 41-66: "Being is through relatedness; but in order that there should be a relation, there must be terms. Thus relatedness presupposes distinctness" (p. 43).

31. G. F. Else, "The Terminology of the Ideas," *Harvard Studies in Classical Philology*, XLVII (1936), 45.

32. *Symposium* 211e 1.

33. *Theaetetus* 205d 1.

tor.[34] What the good dialectician must do is follow the natural distinctions of nature (διαφυή),[35] discover its limbs (μέλη),[36] trace its jointings (ἄρθρα).[37] Clarity, definition, distinction, self-identity are part and parcel of the Greek mind; but nowhere are these virtues more eminent than in Plato. The whole process of the dividing of a thing according to the distinct inner realities that form it is another example of the same desire to grasp self-identities. λόγον δοῦναι, to give an account of a thing, is to be able to block it off from all others and to locate its separate factors.

As for the indivisibility of the Ideas, this is a very complex question indeed, and the matter will not begin to be resolved in a satisfactory way until the close of the third hypothesis. Nevertheless, this opening hypothesis must be taken as an affirmation (over against any kind of multiplicity that may be discovered in the Idea by the process of definition through διαίρεσις) of the fundamental indivisibility of these transcendent factors.

It is clear from the very earliest vocabulary of Plato that the Idea is a *one* of some sort; it is habitually called τὸ ἕν[38] or τὸ ἓν ἐπὶ πολλῶν. It is the unique common fact that pervades any group of particulars and, as thus used, it is not to be confused with *the* Idea of One nor with the original monistic conception of Parmenides.[39] *Each* Idea is a *one*.

34. Else, *loc. cit.*

35. *Politicus* 259d.

36. *Ibid.*, 287c.

37. *Phaedrus* 265e. On the use of these words, see Cherniss, I, 252-53.

38. For a review of the Platonic use of other equivalent phrases, see Else, *op. cit.*, pp. 52 *et circa.*

39. It is Cherniss' opinion (I, 94-95) that Aristotle did so confuse the issue.

Though it is one with regard to a class of particulars, it is not, therefore, immediately clear that it is internally one, that is to say, an indivisible fact. For might it not be a collection, an addition, a mixture of components that are common to a class? No, for Plato also regards them as pure units[40] and this is being said again obliquely in Hypothesis I. And if it is objected that surely there is some kind of composition in them, the only possible answer is that this is a general difficulty for all the *ones* of every order and that the process of solution in the case of the Ideas, and in every case, is revealed in the progress of the logic of the first three hypotheses.

In the first hypothesis, there is a preliminary affirmation of complete indivisibility as at least a factor in any true entity; in the second, it is recognized that each such entity is a whole composed of multiple elements; in the third, it is therefore necessary, over against this evidence for multiplicity, to win our way back in a new way to the rediscovery, through the doctrine of participation, of the original statement of oneness and indivisibility. But meantime we have no reason to question the fact that Plato is here expressing his belief in the absolute indivisibility of the Ideas. And in no case must we be disturbed by the appearance, or the fact, of the multiple entering into anything that may truly be regarded as a separate *entity*. It remains an indivisible for all that.

Plato himself is often fond of using what might be called

40. Cherniss (I, 40) cites the following passages: *Phaedo* 78d; *Symposium* 211a, e; *Republic* 476a; *Philebus* 59c; *Timaeus* 52a.

the "historical-compositional" method of describing an entity. He likes to break down simple entities into "stages of development," even though historically there were no such stages — or into acts of composition, even though in actuality no such *processes* are involved. Thus it is extremely dubious if in the *Republic* he intended us to understand that the final complex political state really passed through the simple stages he there[41] enumerates. And it is almost inconceivable that in the *Timaeus*[42] the "receptacle" of matter, Nurse and Mother of all Becoming, should have pre-existed the entry of the forms into it. Such, too, is the case with the relation between the limit and the unlimited in the *Philebus*.[43] But I shall go into this problem in greater detail in later sections of this book.[44]

This historical-compositional method has been designed by Plato to help us understand essences, hardly to give us a crude metaphysics or politics or geometry or arithmetic[45] or

41. 369 ff.

42. 50c ff.

43. 23c 9 ff.

44. See pp. 222 ff.

45. It is interesting to observe how even the question of arithmetic and the nature of number touches on our present problem. We gather from Aristotle's criticism (*Metaphysics* 1082a 26 ff.) that for Plato each number, as each Idea, is a separate and indivisible reality that is not composed of separate units. For the Academy (cf. *Metaphysics* 1096a 17 ff.) the ideal numbers were not formed by addition. But Aristotle is scarcely in high favor for his arithmetical theory. "The simple truth is that *no* 'number' is 'made of 1's,' and that it is precisely what Aristotle calls 'mathematical' number which has no existence except in his imagination. Plato may well have been led to this denial that numbers are 'addible' by his recognition that 'surds' like $\sqrt{2}$, $\sqrt[3]{2}$ must be admitted into arithmetic, since it is evident that no process of 'adding 1 and 1' could ever yield such numbers as these" —cf. Alfred Edward Taylor, *Plato, The Man and His Work* (New York:

psychology[46] such as would be intolerable to sophisticated minds. The metaphysical unity of the essences under analysis is not meant to be destroyed thereby. In many of the instances of "process" division that have been cited, we are dealing with the Platonic habit of myth-making. But these myths are eminently practical and pedagogical and are not intended to take the place of metaphysics. Rather, myth in the dialogues is not "une méthode pour chercher *le vrai* . . . mais il est une méthode pour exposer *des vraisemblances*. . . ."[47]

1927), p. 507. But Cornford (*Parmenides*, p. 60) has adverse materials to add to this picture.

46. A similar situation emerges from the mythical treatment to which Plato subjects his doctrine of the soul. Is there a tripartite soul in the dialogues? Any literal acceptance of the great myths on this theme would convince us that there is. Cf. the analogy with the tripartite state in *Republic* 368d ff., with the chariot and horses in *Phaedrus* 246a ff., and with the actual localization of the parts of the soul in three different parts of the body in *Timaeus* 87a. And add earlier hints of such a division in the *Phaedo* — cf. John Burnet, *The Phaedo* (Oxford: 1925), note to 68c 2, and the *Gorgias* 493a, b. Though we may observe here that by far the most famous of the Platonic similes, that of the boat and pilot, occurs nowhere in Plato. Despite all these myths, however, extreme doubt exists as to whether this is the final philosophical position of Plato. Note, for example, how much the earlier triple distinction depends on the opposition between bodily and spiritual forces. Yet later, in the *Phaedrus* (246a ff.), we gather that a triple division exists *before* the descent of the soul to earth in bodily form, and that the division may really be based on the triple *direction* of the one reality. Then again, another argument for multiplicity is the radical difference between sensation and intellection (*Phaedo* 80b, 83b; *Republic* 476 ff.; *Timaeus* 51d ff.). But *e contra*, if we are to judge from the *Philebus* (34a), sensation is a common act of soul and body (*ἑνὶ πάθει*). The same soul, therefore, is generating both sensation and intellection. The original crude distinction is further broken down in the *Theaetetus* (185b, 185e 1-2) with its demand for a non-material instrument of thought to perceive the *κοινά of the senses*. Finally, we may recur to the classical lines of the *Republic* (611a ff.) which formally raise the possibility of the soul as a unity if freed of all the seaweed of this life.

47. Léon Robin, *Platon* (Paris: 1935), p. 192.

Therefore, wherever original and absolute unities are broken down into components, whether by definition, addition, mixture, history, or myth, we as philosophers must be careful to preserve the original and paradoxal unity of the fact under discussion. Over against perhaps all the other dialogues, the eight hypotheses of the *Parmenides* are pure metaphysics; it is their business to give a careful summary of the factuality of the indivisible and the multiple in every Idea and every *one* in any order of being — in such a way that oneness is not cancelled by multiplicity. And every myth or mythological tendency in the dialogues must, therefore, be thrown up against the philosophical accuracies of the *Parmenides:* the metaphysical niceties of the latter must be taken as limits that may not be violated by any other searching instrument of the human person.[48] But at the present moment we are

48. The limitations under which every other such instrument labors are clearly recognized and defined by Plato himself, and it is he who is responsible for the first attempt at a scientific fixing of the limits of the different "faculties" of man. The "divided line" of the *Republic* (509d ff.) is a general appraisal of the relation of all such faculties to the truth. A good deal of the *Meno*, *Protagoras*, and *Theaetetus* is devoted to indicating the knowledge-limits of δόξα, or unscientific opinion (e.g., *Meno* 83 *circa*). "Popular" virtue is a limited ethics because it is not philosophically aware of ends and purposes (e.g., *Phaedo* 68d ff.). The *Ion* and *Apology* criticize the deficiencies of poetic intuition. Pleasure and pain are another species of short-sighted seeing (e.g., *Phaedo* 83c, d). Cf. also *Republic* 561c; *Gorgias* 494e-495a; *Philebus* 13; *Protagoras* 353d; *Laws* 733. The *Gorgias* (465a) puts experience and the "experimental" in its lower place in the ladder of knowledge. But we must understand that all the physical sciences are for Plato only approximations to the truth and partake therefore of the nature of myth. And in this respect it has been pointed out that he is a much more modest scientist than Aristotle — cf. Taylor, *A Commentary on Plato's Timaeus* (Oxford: 1928), p. 135. The whole scientific system of the *Timaeus* is as factual as a scientist of that period can make it, but its author still describes the whole of it as mythical (*Timaeus* 24d,

faced with an insistence on the total simplicity of the Idea; on the contrary, there is no other text in the whole Platonic corpus that more clearly needs to be so read as to rule out any such simplicity.

Ideas and Sensibles Related

Again, if our reading is correct, another crucially important principle emerges for Platonic metaphysics. The One under analysis is a *one* that may be found in any order of the real and, wherever you have unity, the resulting analysis is admissible. It is not, therefore, in the order of essential or conceptual analysis that one Platonic order differs from another. There is indeed a profound difference between the world of true being (or the Ideas) and that of becoming.[49] But as a

29c, 30b, 36a, 40c, 44c, 48c, 48d, 54d, 68b, 69a, b, 72d, 90c; these are texts collected by Taylor). For a study of the values and limitations of the analogical relationship of mathematical thinking to philosophy in Plato, cf. Robert S. Brumbaugh, *Plato's Mathematical Imagination* (Bloomington, 1954). Brumbaugh's excellent note on mathematics as hypothetical science (p. 280, n. 29 for chap. III) should be carefully read.

49. I myself am convinced that Plato held unfailingly to a belief in the transcendental existence of the Ideas. For a brief study of the problem, cf. Cherniss, I, 206 ff., especially notes 123 and 124. Aristotle himself held to the view that Plato had located the Ideas in a transcendent world, and he therefore concluded that they must always possess transcendent qualities in whatever order he (Aristotle) chose thereafter to find them intermingled. It is unnecessary to elaborate the central quarrel that still goes on over this attribution of the pure, other-worldly status to the Ideas. The Kantians, of course, would reject it. Others would hold that transcendence is a crude materialization of a noble concept. Constantin Ritter (*The Essence of Plato's Philosophy* [London: 1933]) would restrict the Ideas entirely to the world of Becoming and would define them as the objective ground of scientific judgments. He explains the later avoidance by Plato of the word "Idea" by saying that it carried with it such associations of eternal im-

matter of fact the *Timaeus*[50] establishes only one difference between Ideas and particulars, that between eternity and time; in all other ways they are alike. But this is entirely an existential distinction and refers rather to two different modes of achieving the same essence. This means that what is permanently, immutably, and co-instantaneously accomplished in eternity is achieved through the divisible and growing processes of space and time in particulars. For an example, let us take the biological growth of man. This growth has a fixed pattern and has its own uniqueness and unity. In the order of Becoming, this pattern, like a musical melody, is spread out in space and time. Its elements are not co-instantaneous. But in eternity the end of the process is co-instantaneous with its beginning. Another way of saying the same thing is to say that every spatial and temporal feature of a given law of motion is eternally set and eternally true.

In a word, we are not to suppose that the approximation, the aspiration, the "tendency toward," of particulars in relation to Ideas are approximations to the notion defining the Idea essentially; rather they tend toward the purity of its transcendent status. Thus, as early as this in the history of philosophy we are given a *theory of analogy:*[51] the same con-

---

mutability and absolute separateness as could no longer satisfy the author of the *Sophist*, the *Statesman*, etc. (see especially p. 111 *et circa*). Many scholastic philosophers seem to be frightened by the concept of an eternal man or horse floating around as an eternal model, but surely this does small justice to the Platonic notion. On the other hand, there are philosophers who would hold that Aristotle, by surrendering the Platonic notion of some form of transcendent essences, made metaphysics impossible. Certainly the whole question is not a primitive one, but is crucial still to all philosophy.

50. 37d.

51. For a sympathetic treatment of the varied presence of a doctrine of analogy in Plato, see Paul Grenet's book, *Les Origines de l'analogie*

cept is present in the two orders; the mode of achievement is profoundly different. Such a principle preserves the absolute difference between being and Becoming, a difference that can never be bridged existentially; but at the same time it preserves the unity of the two orders and deals effectively enough with the dilemma that God cannot know our world and we cannot know his. He who knows analytically or by divine seeing what unity is knows it for what it must be in any field of the real.

---

philosophique dans les dialogues de Platon (Paris: 1948). For a critique of Grenet in Thomistic terms, see the review by James F. Anderson in "Analogy in Plato," *The Review of Metaphysics*, IV (1950), 111-28.

4

THE CONCLUDING LINES OF HYPOTHESIS I

(*141d-142a*)

The Problems:

The concluding lines of Hypothesis I are really a brief outline of a key doctrine in Platonic epistemology. No completely indivisible principle can be known in terms of ἐπιστήμη, or formally scientific knowledge; it is even clearer that it cannot be the object of sensation or opinion. For that matter, neither can being be so known, or a pure element, or the unlimited, or non-being. This does not mean that none of these exists. And thus we avoid giving a purely negative sense to Hypothesis I.

4

These are the concluding propositions of the first hypothesis, around which center some of the severest problems of interpretation in the *Parmenides:*

A *one* does not exist in time at all.
A *one* does not have past, present, or future time, neither was nor is nor shall be.
A *one,* therefore, has no share in being; it is not.
A *one,* therefore, is not even one.
A *one,* then, has neither name nor definition, nor is there knowledge, sensation, or opinion of it.
But it is impossible that all this be true of the one. Let us therefore start all over again!

This conclusion seems on the face of it to leave unassailable the anti-Eleatic interpretation of the whole dialogue. In brief, we are given a denial of any possible predication for the *oneness* of this hypothesis; as a climax we discover that it cannot even be said to *be* and cannot even receive a judgment of self-identity: the *one* is not even one and it does not have a name; of it there cannot be either knowledge or perception or opinion. If, then, we are to make any true progress we must retrace our steps and begin all over again. What more apt lines could have been written for those who view the *Parmenides* as an assault by Plato on the whole metaphysical position of Parmenides?

And to lend still further credence, if that were necessary, to the very general impression among the commentators that Hypothesis I has ended in purely negative results, while Hypothesis II alone begins to yield any positive sense, we may now cite the counter-reading at the close of the latter:[1]

A *one* now partakes of time.
A *one* was, is, and shall be.
A *one* is in relationship to things, in past, present, and future.
There is now knowledge, opinion, and perception of the one.
A *one* now has a name and can be defined.

The facile thing at this point would be to yield to the obvious strength of these contrasting tests and to acknowledge what seems quite clear: that at the end of Hypothesis I Plato has an unnamable monster on his hands in the shape of a pure and indivisible *one* that cannot even exist. Apart from the Neoplatonists, I believe this is a universal conclusion. Certainly, if there is no other plausible understanding of these final lines than that of the Neoplatonists or the anti-Eleatics, what we have said so far of the meaning of the dialogue must be rejected. But I should like to offer an altogether different reading of the passage.

1. 155c, d.

The Concluding Lines of Hypothesis I

The major difficulty here is that these lines have been isolated and have not been studied in the light of the whole dialogue. More important still, they have not been examined in the light of the habits of expression that characterize the whole Platonic corpus. If they are understood aright, nothing of the achievement we have gathered in the previous pages for the first hypothesis will be lost and these concluding lines will be seen as of the utmost transitional importance for a further positive achievement in the ensuing hypotheses. The evidence for such a view may be summed up under three headings:

1. The first point is a very simple one. If we were immediately to accept the purely negative force of the conclusion to Hypothesis I, then consistency would demand that we do the same for the conclusions of a good number of the other dialogues. This would also hold for the closing lines of the *Parmenides* itself — for they are completely destructive in their tone.[2]

The word "irony," of course, quickly suggests itself. Plato

2. Consistency is a virtue for the interpreter, and it would be welcomed in this particular problem. We may suspect that sometimes a commentator accepts lines as ironic if such a view helps his case, or rejects the possibility of irony where it does not. For example, Cornford takes Plato's concluding lines in Hypothesis I quite literally because he views that hypothesis as completely negative. He thereafter proceeds to build out of the remainder of the *Parmenides* a positive system of metaphysics. When he comes to the closing lines of the dialogue, which describe all that has preceded as a complete mass of contradictions, it suits his purpose to remark: "That this conclusion is only ostensible will now be clear to any reader who accepts the principles of the foregoing interpretation as even approximately correct. . . . It is a challenge to the student. . . . This is no new device in Plato. . . . In a whole series of the early dialogues . . . the conclusion that is meant to be accepted is skillfully masked, so that the reader may be forced to discover it by careful study" (*Parmenides*, pp. 244-45).

surely knew what irony was, has formally defined it as "saying less than one thinks,"[3] and has often used it.[4] Much, therefore, may have been accomplished even where a man says he has accomplished nothing. And this is a possible explanation for the specific conclusion we are now discussing.

Yet we must add that it is not a perfectly accurate explanation and is too pretty a way out of our dilemma. For one thing, it is to be feared that the Platonic use of irony is, at least on some occasions, a far more complex process than the above description would indicate.

We must not imagine that in every case Plato is equivalently saying: do not take my negative and discouraging finale seriously; in reality my waiver of positive results is only the way a modest man boasts. This would be a severe over-simplification of his irony. Rather, the truth is an interesting situation in which considerable positive progress has been won but in which some kind of an impasse has also been met. In brief, the irony and the boast are there, but it is not all irony.

The *Lysis* may be alleged as a perfect example of this kind of complex attitude. Indeed, it is so good an example and will so greatly illuminate the present issue that it is worth pausing here to examine it in some detail.

The dialogue is really, though of course not nominally, an essay on the tortuous Greek problem of *becoming*. Actually, though implicitly, it starts from the Parmenidean conviction

3. *Republic* 337a.

4. For example, cf. *Charmides* 175a, b; *Protagoras* 361a, b; *Lysis* 222d, e. For Xenophon on Socratic irony, see *Memorabilia* IV. 2. 39, and for Aristotle on the use of the word, see *Nichomachean Ethics* II . vii . 12.

that from being nothing comes — for it already is — and from non-being nothing comes — for how can anything come of it? Therefore becoming or change is impossible. These are the principles or dilemmas which guide the search of the *Lysis* for a definition of τὸ φίλον, or "the friendly."

To what is a thing friendly? To what does it attach itself? And for these we might substitute the questions: Toward what does a thing move? Into what does it grow? Not toward the "like" (for it already has and is what is like to itself).[5] Nor toward the "unlike" (for how can the unlike come out of that which is absolutely not itself?).[6] No, a thing is friendly toward that of which it has a "lack" (ἐνδεές)[7] and this is not any kind of lack but a relation to a determined object. It is what Aristotle would call ἀδυναμία διορισθεῖσα, a determinate lack or potency.[8] This relationship of ἔνδεια, Plato says, is toward what is proper, or οἰκεῖον.[9] But how can there be a deprivation and a desire of the οἰκεῖον that, of its very nature, is "like"? Are we thus back where we began and has the whole dialogue, plus the possibility of desire and motion, collapsed?[10] Yes and no. No — because I believe the substantials of the whole Aristotelian solution of the possibility of change are here achieved. Yes — because Plato is being more honest than Aristotle in recognizing a final impasse that every metaphysics of motion must face: that which is sought or moved towards is somehow already possessed. This dilemma is recognizably true even of the στέρησις of Aristotle, for it is itself already

5. *Lysis* 214e.
6. *Lysis* 216a, b.
7. *Ibid.*, 221e.
8. *Metaphysics* 1055b 7-8.
9. *Lysis* 221e 3-4.
10. *Ibid.*, 222d 1-3.

the form toward which it moves.[11] He acknowledges the difficulty but glides over it rapidly.

Here, then, is a more complicated extension to the term "irony" for Plato. It means what it says, yet it does not. A solidly progressive argument has marched to a systematic conclusion and yet a real difficulty remains. The same situation is now repeating itself in the *Parmenides*. We shall shortly see what the nature of the impasse is, but now suffice it to say that not a word of what has preceded is annulled.

2. The second point is one that has been cited before.[12] It cannot be fully verified at the moment but must be held in mind until we reach the second hypothesis. It is simply this: a careful reading of this subsequent hypothesis will reveal that the positive conclusions it does actually reach depend

11. See *Physics* 193b 19-20 (καὶ γὰρ ἡ στέρησις εἶδός πώς 'εστιν), and again *Metaphysics* 1055b 7-8 (ἀδυναμία διορισθεῖσα). On this particular point, see Cherniss, *Aristotle's Criticism of Presocratic Philosophy* (footnote 255, page 62). Simplicius, *In Aristotelis Phys. libros commentaria* (as edited by Hermann Diels), *in* 280 . 12-22, gives us various reasons why στέρησις is in a sense a form, or εἶδος: (a) because it is present in a ὑποκείμενον and characterizes it, as εἶδος also does; (b) because it is not a mere absence of form, but absence of form in something that might have the form — and fitness to receive the privation is a sort of corrupted form; (c) because certain privations may be considered as the inferior of two contrary forms, and because either of the two contrary forms is the privation of the other. The same difficulty, by the way, is encountered in the concept of matter of Plotinus. Cf. René Arnou, *Le désir de Dieu dans la philosophie de Plotin* (Paris: 1921), pp. 72-73: "Aussi, bien qu'il dise et répète après Aristote que la matière est 'privee de toute détermination' . . . , qu'elle n'est pas un corps . . . , étant ἄποιος, mais seulement en puissance, il ne peut s'en tenir à cette sévère conception, 'il jette' lui aussi sur elle 'le manteau de la forme' . . . un minimum de détermination, assez cependant pour en faire 'une chose' . . ."

12. See chap. 5, n. 1. I repeat that such texts as are referred to in this later note are very important in indicating that Plato is being faithful in the second hypothesis to the logic we have proposed as being present in the first.

largely upon the positive metaphysical doctrine which we have proposed as the content of Hypothesis I. As we shall discover, it is hereafter essential that, at least in concept, a *one* as one be only one and be not confused even with the notion of being. In general, then, there will be no retracing of steps at all. The next hypothesis simply "goes on from there," so to speak.

3. With the third point, however, we really approach the heart of the matter and discover the ultimate reason for our negative ending:

When Plato tells us that there can be no "knowledge" of such a thing as the *one* of the first hypothesis, we must be careful not to draw the wrong conclusion from such a statement. It is clear to every student of the dialogues that the word "knowledge" can be a highly technical term in the vocabulary of Plato, as can a number of other epistemological terms.[13] What the Master of the Academy here has reference to is that scientific type of knowledge that is the object of analysis for the *Theaetetus*,[14] and it does not follow

13. For a study of the growth of a technical philosophical terminology in the dialogues, see Benjamin Jowett and Lewis Campbell, *Plato's Republic* (Oxford: 1894), II, 291 ff.

14. The most precise and elaborate effort to define ἐπιστήμη, or true knowledge, will be found in the *Theaetetus*. There, following the usual hypothetical method, we progress through three attempts at definition: (a) sensation (151e-187b); (b) true opinion (187b-201d); (c) true opinion of a reality accompanied by an "account" of it — δόξα ἀληθής μετὰ λόγου (201e-210a). The problem, of course, is the meaning of the word λόγος. For a well-drawn distinction between the λόγος of the *Theaetetus* and the λόγος or λογισμός of the *Meno*, *Phaedo*, and *Symposium*, see A. Diès, *Autour de Platon* (Paris: 1927), pp. 465 ff. I myself feel, however, that the *Parmenides* itself is no small contribution to the Platonic attempt at defining scientific or philosophic knowledge.

that because a thing cannot be the object of such knowledge it therefore does not *exist*. For the sake of complete clarity we should take this occasion to restate the major theme of the *Parmenides* up to the present moment.

The first part of the dialogue had ended with the insistence, against every assault, that there must be Ideas and that the whole possibility of human language and philosophy depends upon them. In entire consonance with this position, the first hypothesis has opened the dialectical defense of the Ideas by asserting the existence of absolutely unique, separate factors that can in no way be confused one with the other. Whether these separate factors are found in their pure form in the transcendent Ideas, or in the shape of human definitions of the same, or in the participating mode of visible objects, we can apply to them practically all the qualities or negations of the Parmenidean or Neoplatonic One. There is an element in everything truly a "thing" that is simple and undivided. So true is this that such an element will not share the divisibilities of space and time even when it is located in the order of space and time. Such indivisible factors can and must exist. Therefore the first hypothesis rightly begins with such a doctrine.

But it is entirely another thing to say that these factors can be known as such, known in their sheer indivisibility and simplicity. A *one*, precisely as one, is not "known" as such by the rational mind, which, we shall see, always knows in terms of the one and multiple.[15] *De facto*, there can be and there is

15. Demos puts this truth acutely ("The One and the Many in Plato," pp. 54-55): "Plato points out that if knowledge is an analysis of a complex into its elements, then the complex must be either the totality of its parts, or a whole with an indivisible unity. If the former, then, since the elements

real knowledge of things — and that in the highest Platonic sense of the word. But this is only possible because there are in things more than absolutely unifying factors. The existence of the latter has been asserted by common sense and philosophical intuition in the first half of the dialogue. Thereafter, in the first hypothesis, elaborate dialectic has added to this assertion the most exhaustive description of the simple Ideas that is to be found so far in the dialogues. But it will be the business of the second hypothesis to discover those further principles in essences that bring them into the range of human knowledge. Our paradox, however, will remain: that, no matter what the multiplicity now entering the picture, the pure One survives it all.[16]

A brief excursion on one of the problems of human knowledge is here necessary. It may be summarized by saying that

---

are unknown, so will the complex be unknown. If the latter, then the complex, which is indivisible, is simply another element, and unknowable like the primary constituents. The fallacy which Plato has in mind would seem to be that we are defining knowledge as a mechanical rather than an organic system. We are conceiving of the perception of the elements as already there, antecedently to their ingredience in the complex act of knowledge; and so we construe the complex act in terms of the simple acts. Yet the simple acts do not exist save in their relation to the synthesis. There is no static knowledge, even of elements; all knowledge is relational. . . ." For another excellent description of the object and nature of Platonic "knowledge," cf. Halévy, *La Théorie platonicienne des sciences*, pp. 190-92.

16. Cf. H. Cherniss, I, 40-41: "The possible argument that in the employment of diaeresis Plato neglected or abandoned the indivisible unity of the idea is precluded by the implications of Aristotle's own criticism (*Metaphysics* 1045a 17-20) . . . after analyzing the idea into constituent elements he (Aristotle) declares the unified substance to be superfluous. His own words, however, show that according to this theory men (*for example*) are organized wholes just because they participate in the unitary substantiality of a single idea."

the pure, undivided essence or form or Idea or thing is in no case the "proper object" of the human intellect. And this point is the larger burden of the thought of the first two hypotheses. This principle must be pressed much further to recognize the full import of all that is involved. Nothing that is purely simple or single is the object of the human mind.[17] A *one* as such is not within its competence. A keen introspective faculty makes Plato aware of the multiple and rationalizing character of the human intelligence — for which the vision of absolute unity in any order is an impossible feat. Indeed, there are two things that are not within our range. They are pure unity and pure multiplicity.[18] And that this is thoroughly Platonic may be verified from a careful examination of all those things in the dialogues to which Plato denies the possibility of true knowledge. This knowledge will always have as its object a one-many. It would be too long a parenthesis to run in adequate detail through all the separate problems which this simple principle creates in the various dialogues. Perhaps it is enough to cite a list of such problems in the briefest way and to hope that such a listing will throw light on our present difficulty.

The Unknowable in Plato

a. The Good is above all our knowing and there can be no scientific knowledge of it. It is the source of all essence but it

17. Aquinas puts the matter very succinctly, in the following way: "Ratio ad formam simplicem pertingere non potest, ut sciat de ea quid est. Potest tamen de ea cognoscere, ut sciat an est." (*Summa Theologica* 1.12.12 *ad* 1. Cf. also 1.13.12 *ad* 2, 3 and 1.14.14)

18. "Unité pure et pluralité pure sont le néant d'être et le néant de pensée." (Auguste Diès, *op. cit.*, p. 480.)

differs from every essence in that it cannot be comprehended as they can.[19] Because of such phrasing as this in the lines of the *Republic* that deal with the Good, the Neoplatonists even in our day equate the One of the first hypothesis and the Idea of the Good in the *Republic*.[20] They still fail to recognize that similar phrasing is discoverable in a number of dialogues dealing with altogether different subjects. This similarity is always due to the presence of a common epistemological principle. There can be no scientific knowledge of strict unity and no such knowledge of strict multiplicity.

b. The single, indivisible *elements* (στοιχεῖα) of anything are unknowable. It is impossible to define, or give an account

19. For the great Platonic hymn to the Good and analysis of it, see *Republic* 505a ff. See also the seventh *Epistle* 341c, e. It is impossible here to summarize Plato's complete doctrine of the good, which runs in a complicated way through many of the dialogues. For example, practically all the definitions of particular virtues in the earlier dialogues finally end in an encounter with the good. In the practical order the good is the end of every desire (*Meno* 77b, c; *Gorgias* 499e; *Protagas* 358b; *Republic* 505d); it is also the final end of every action (*Gorgias* 499e: Τέλος εἶναι ἁπασῶν τῶν πράξεων τὸ ἀγαθόν). Whether it is for Plato completely identical with the nature of God is not an easy matter to determine. A good note on the subject is contained in a review of Friedrich Solmsen's *Plato's Theology* by E. Frank in the *American Journal of Philology*, LXVI (January, 1945), 92-96. In the *Gorgias* (506d), the good is identified with the principle of order. In the *Timaeus* (29d, e), it is allied with the idea of communication and the sharing of goods.

20. See Alfred Jules Emile Fouillé, *La Philosophie de Platon* (Paris: 1912), I, 175: "Le premier Principe ne participe pas plus à l'identité qu'à la diversité: il les produit et les limite l'une par l'autre dans la plus parfaite indépendance et sans que son existence absolue connaisse elle-même aucune limite. Dans cette region suprême de la raison pure, les thèses et les antithèses de l'entendement s'évanouissent en une synthèse supérieure; l'un est et n'est pas le même ou autre que ce qu'il produit, soutient, domine." This is an obvious combination of Plotinus and Hegel. Hardie (*A Study in Plato*, p. 123) defends Proclus for his interpretation of the negatives of the first hypothesis.

of such an element. It is not too much to say the reason is basically analogous to that which makes a pure one indefinable. Aristotle himself defines such an element (Στοιχεῖον λέγεται ἐξ οὗ σύγκειται πρώτου ἐνυπάρχοντος ἀδιαιρέτου τῷ εἴδει εἰς ἕτερον εἶδος[21]) and he too would recognize that it is unknowable. The relationship between the elements and the "syllable," not only in language but, analogously, in any form of reality, is one of the key subjects of the *Theaetetus* — as is the knowability of each absolutely and of each as related to the other. And the reason for the unknowability of each as separated from the other is not left obscure. For if, in the ontological order, both the syllable and any element of the same are a *one* and an undivided reality (ἕν τε καὶ ἀμερές),[22] then the epistemological consequence for either is the impossibility of definition or knowledge (ἄλογόν τε καὶ ἄγνωστον).[23] But this is surely the place to repeat our major point. There is not the slightest doubt in the mind of Plato about the objective existence of either "element" or "syllable." No more than there is any question for him of the existence of the absolute and indivisible *one* of Hypothesis I. As a matter of fact, we shall have occasion to see that the doctrine of the *Theaetetus* closely parallels that of the *Parmenides*, for in due time the latter will also declare that the elements of a *one*, conceived separately from a *one*, are unknowable. And this is only a typical example of the constant concordance of the eight hypotheses with the whole body of surrounding dialogues.

c. One of the substantial conclusions of the *Sophist* is that

21. *Metaphysics* 1014a 26.
22. *Theaetetus* 205e 2.
23. *Ibid.*, 205e 3.

being itself is undefinable — and therefore is unknowable in our technical sense. It is the office of the philosopher to determine the proper interplay of separate realities.[24] There are five "categories"[25] of the real: being, motion, rest, same, other. Being is reducible to none of the other categories, though all of them participate in it.[26] It is really impossible to give a strict account (λόγῳ) of it.[27] Aristotle, on his part, would apparently conceive being again as an "element" and, therefore, as a "simple unity" (ἓν . . . καὶ ἁπλοῦν).[28] The consequences of such a status for the knowledge of being will be obvious at once. Yet no one would dare suggest that being does not exist.

d. The "receptacle," or ὑποδοχή of the *Timaeus* provokes a special epistemological question — as does every form of the multiple in Plato. First of all, we are not quite certain what the precise identity of this receptacle, the Mother and Nurse of all becoming, is.[29] It is not too clear that it is the Aristotelian matter, or ὕλη.[30] What is certain is that it is a

24. *Sophist* 253d, e.

25. This word has crept into the vocabulary of Platonic scholarship, though perhaps it has unfortunate connotations.

26. *Sophist* 254d ff.

27. *Ibid.*, 249d 7 *et circa.*

28. *Metaphysics* 1014b 6-7.

29. Is the ὑποδοχή of the *Timaeus* a timeless space capable of receiving all forms and itself possessed of none — the continuum of space? After remarking that "you cannot say what the ὑποδοχή is except by means of negatives," Taylor (in his *Timaeus*) proceeds to give a mathematical interpretation of our subject in terms of some kind of pure extension: "Extension is the continuum implied in the existence of geometrical figures" (pp. 331-32).

30. Aristotle himself identifies the two (*Physics* 192a 13-14). See Cherniss, I, 85 ff.

completely indeterminate principle, without form or unity,[31] and such a principle of complete multiplicity is for Plato neither knowable nor altogether unknowable; it is to be apprehended by a kind of bastard reasoning (λογισμῷ τινι νόθῳ).[32] Now, so far as the *Parmenides* is concerned, the analogue of this kind of reality and the analogue of this kind of semi-knowledge will be found in Hypothesis IV, which is an elaborate description of the infinite, or ἄπειρον present in a *one*.

e. We now come to a final form of unknowability, which in reality is its only absolute form. It is the type that attaches to absolute non-being. The classical quarrel about the nature of non-being and its different forms will be treated in Hypotheses V, VI, and VIII, but in the present instance there can be no misunderstanding. The non-being we here cite exists in no way whatsoever. The ancients agree that there can be no knowledge of it whatsoever.[33] And Plato, of course, agrees with them. Being does not belong to it, nor does number[34]—whether the number be of one or of multitude. It is ἀδιονόητόν τε καὶ ἄρρητον καὶ ἄφθεγκτον καὶ ἄλογον.[35]

Conclusion

In all the above, there is one thing that must emerge with eminent clarity. It is impossible to think that the concept of

31. *Timaeus* 50d ff.

32. *Ibid.*, 52b 2. See also 51a 7-b 1.

33. For example, *Parmenides* Frags. 2 and 3; cf. Hermann Diels, *Die Fragmente der Vorsokratiker* (Berlin: 1954), I, 231 — translations for Diels in Kathleen Freeman, *Ancilla to the Pre-Socratic Philosophers*, (Cambridge: 1948).

34. *Sophist* 238a.

35. *Ibid.*, 238c.

unknowability is being used in the same sense in every case we have introduced. With Plato, knowledge is to be defined in terms of its object, and it is equally certain that the different degrees of knowing derive their status from the different degrees of reality in the object. In that respect, witness the whole parable of the divided line in the *Republic*.[36] Somewhat the same thing holds true of non-knowing. The word "unknowable" may itself indicate different degrees or states of non-existence. Certainly there are different "relations to objects" to be attached to "incomprehensibility" in the case of the indivisible One, the unlimited, and absolute non-being. In the one case there is an absolute but incomprehensible existence, in the second a semi-existence, in the third none at all.

The *one* of the first hypothesis, we conclude, does exist. As such, however, it cannot be known by the *rational* intelligence. If we further analyze the nature of Idea or essence, we will discover further principles in it that bring it into the range of that intelligence. That we do in the following hypothesis.

36. 509d ff.

5

HYPOTHESIS II

The Problems:

Hypothesis I has been responsible for a positive achievement and a real difficulty. It has established complete oneness, or indivisibility, as a principle in all beings; but this principle is not knowable on such pure terms. Hypothesis II, standing midway between the first and third hypotheses — between absolute indivisibility and structured unity — proceeds to study a *one* as a composition of parts.

Whatever the later metaphysical explanation, many things do co-exist in whole entities. Communication, or *κοινωνία*. The indeterminate as foundation for later unity. The limit-unlimited as basis for all other contrarieties. The self-identity of a *one*. The continua of space and time. And many other matters.

5

The simplest way of describing the logical advance of the second over the first hypothesis is to say that oneness now emerges, no longer as a pure indivisible, but as a whole of parts. "Parts" is the Platonic word, though perhaps "members" or "factors" would better serve our purpose and would be less suggestive of a restriction of our logic to sensible parts. Never for a moment does the dialogue abandon the principle that there is an indivisible of pure oneness in every entity of every order,[1] but we now learn that every such *one* also contains a multiplicity of some kind, whether sensible, numerical, conceptual, or transcendent. Throughout this hypothesis and all those that follow (with the possible exception of the fifth), this multiple element of many factors will be described by the name of the "others" or "other."[2]

1. In a word, nothing that follows alters the achievement of Hypothesis I. Indeed, there is a constantly recurring note in the second hypothesis that, no matter how multiple a *one* has become, it still remains an indivisible; the concept of a *one* as nothing but *one* remains and is basic for all the dialectic that follows. I have never seen any attention paid to such later texts as the following: 143a 8-b 7, 145e 8-146a 2, 146c 3-4, all of which fortify this point.

2. Azary Weber, *Essai sur la deuxième hypothèse du Parménide* (Paris: 1937), p. 17, would *always* equate "the Others" with the content of the sensible order over against the Ideas: "Quant aux Autres, je dis qu'ils

It is also possible to say that the subject of the second hypothesis is that of communion, or κοινωνία. But this actually is the same as saying that a *one* is a whole. Up to now, our first metaphysical analysis of any unity has revealed it as an isolated entity that is without division and that of itself enters into no relation with any other entity inside or outside of it. Now we become aware that a number of such units can coalesce to form a large unit, and this will serve as our first rough description of what κοινωνία means: the ability of any two or more factors so to relate themselves that coexistence in a whole is possible. This is by no means all that Plato will have to say about the nature of communion or relation. Indeed, as we shall see, all the succeeding hypotheses, save the fifth, can very well be understood as serving the function of refining the Platonic notion of κοινωνία, or the coexistence of things. And even Hypothesis V deals in a negative way with the same metaphysical problem, for, with its analysis of the Platonic concept of *otherness*, it is really discovering the principle that forbids the community of certain elements and makes distinction possible between *ones* and within *ones*.

In brief, Hypothesis II comes to the following general conclusions: (1) any one thing is really a complexus of ele-

---

égalent le devenir sensible, c'est-à-dire l'un-qui-est." Parts of the evidence he gives for this opinion are very interesting: "Car, si l'Un figure souvent l'Idée, le mot Autres parait être fréquement employé pour designer les choses sensibles qui en participent . . . et justement la première partie du Parménide donne ce sens au moins six fois (130e; 131e; 132a; 132c; 132d; 133a)." But all this seems to reopen an old and endless question. For words such as *one* (ἕν) and all its correlates can just as well themselves refer in the dialogues to the sensible (cf. Else, "The Terminology of the Ideas," p. 40 *circa*) and this writer could just as well select a use of the phrase τὰ ἄλλα from the first half of the *Parmenides* (129c 1), which clearly has reference to the world of Ideas.

ments or parts and these constitute a whole, one element of which is indivisible, the other divisible (a one-many); (2) further exploration reveals that the parts to be discovered in a *one* are infinite; in reality, then, the constituting elements of a *one* are the limit and unlimited; this is a fundamental contrariety rooted in all being and is the source for the ascription of all other contraries to any unity;[3] (3) from this fundamental contrariety proceed a number of others: in itself — in another; moving — at rest; same — different; like — unlike; equal — unequal; (4) the two basic elements of one-many, indivisible-divisible, limit-unlimited, are then put to special use in solving the antinomies of the spatial and temporal continua.

Thus the hypothesis goes further than being a study of the possibility of the co-existence of factors within unified wholes; it will, for example, be but a minor part of its work to show that there is such a communion between oneness and being. Its more difficult task is to establish the κοινωνία of *contrary* elements in all being, and in this it begins to fulfill the implicit promises made in the first half of the dialogue.[4] At the same time, the hypothesis must not be conceived as going further than it actually does. It is quite satisfied to establish the *co-presence* of contraries in a *one* and to leave to succeeding sections the more subtle explication of the metaphysical *relations between* such elements as the one and many

3. For a summary of the manner in which the Pythagoreans established the same fundamental contrariety and listed other pairs under them, see William David Ross, *Aristotle's Metaphysics* (Oxford: 1924), I, 148 ff. For Aristotle himself (*Metaphysics* 1054a 29), the terms same, like, equal belong to the *one;* the terms other, unlike, unequal belong to plurality.

4. 129d, e; 135e.

or the limit and unlimited. For example, we shall have later occasion to see that it is not quite true to say that there is in any *one* a one *and* a many, a limit *and* an unlimited. In Hypothesis III and VIII, the one, or principle of unity, will emerge as the exclusive source both of predication and existence for its members, and will thus avoid being confronted with a *strict* division or multiplicity of elements in being. I indicate so much at this point only to stress once again the fundamental reliance of Plato on the Eleatic logic. Here, in the second hypothesis, that system is being corrected to allow for multiple elements in every order of reality.

Another brief review of the eight hypotheses as a *progressive* definition or "account" (λόγος) of the nature of unity may help to sharpen the difference between mere co-presence of elements and the inter-relationship of elements:

Different features of unity are analyzed in different hypotheses. Thus the first has dissected the question of a *one* precisely as it is one and nothing but one. The second will now discover that each *one* is a whole constituted of a one and many, of a limit and unlimited; the third, much more subtle than its predecessor, that the *many* (i.e., all the single elements of the whole) ultimately derive their definiteness as single factors from the one or limit in a thing. The fourth will give us an "account" of this unlimited element of manyness, for, apart from the one, the many are indefinite and unlimited. In the fifth hypothesis, we shall discover that any unity contains an element of relation — to be called non-being or difference or otherness — by which it is distinguished from all other *ones*. The study of absolute non-being in Hypothesis VI helps to sharpen our understanding of the relative non-being of V. So far, then, we have a philosophical analysis of the elements of unity and their relation to each other. In Hypothesis VII, however, we are given a philosophical study of δόξα, or of the non-philosophical view of a *one*, which always runs into confusion because it does not perceive the element of unity present in any complex whole. Finally, Hypothesis VIII is climactic: if there is no unity in a being, then nothing in it exists. This is equivalent to saying that not only is the principle of unity the source of definite predicability for the parts of a whole (cf. III); it is also the source of their very being. Strictly speaking, therefore, there *is* only a *one;* its parts only exist by *participation* in the being of this unity, and not, so to speak, as co-absolutes with that unity.

In other words, it will finally be by a more subtle application of the doctrine of "participation" (μέθεξις), and by its application to the internal structure of all unities, in all orders, that Plato will resolve many of the antinomies at the heart of being, principal among which are the co-existing phenomena of oneness and manyness. Μέθεξις will no longer be a doctrine restricted to describing the relation between Ideas and their particular instances. Somewhat the same process is followed in the *Sophist* where, however, it is *being* and not oneness that is subject to a fresh analysis. There, being will emerge not only as a special γένος on a par with same-other, motion-rest; it will also be a whole within which all these major γένη exist by participation in it and in each other. As in Aristotle, then, there is in Plato a clear-cut concept of absolute and relative existence in every entity, though we must not confuse the absolute element in Plato with the notion of substance in Aristotle. Nor must we, in Plato, completely identify the two doctrines of κοινωνία and μέθεξις. Κοινωνία is a word used to describe any kind of co-existence of elements; μέθεξις, or participation, is a much more refined notion and is used to explain the absolute-derivative relation according to which the one and many, or being and its elements, co-exist. And the interesting thing is that the word "participation" is now also being used to indicate the relation between Ideas themselves.

Another reason for this further, brief review of all the hypotheses before we engage ourselves in the detail of the second is in order once again to remove a false impression about any or all of the hypotheses. None of them is negative or impossible in its conclusions; none of them results in contradictions that are solved by later hypotheses. Most of them are complete statements about single qualities of a unity or elements within it. There is no constant Hegelian progression of separate falsehood of thesis and anti-thesis into the truth of synthesis. Each hypothesis is a full account of a separate problem of unity. At the end we have a complete definition of a *one*. But this definition is not to be found in the eighth; it is to be found in the sum of all eight hypotheses.

The Text of Hypothesis II
(*142b-155d*)

The following are the conclusions arrived at in Hypothesis II. It is clear that they form a body of propositions directly at odds, or so it would seem, with the first hypothesis. Everything that is there denied of a *one* is here affirmed. I have again taken the liberty of dividing the series of statements according to the general division of their subject matter.

Divisibility	A *one* has being.
	A *one* is a whole of parts.
	A *one* has an infinite element in it.
Articulation	A *one* is limited.
	A *one* has a beginning, a middle, and an end.
Figure	A *one* is straight or round or both.
Place	A *one* is in itself and in the Others.
Motion	A *one* is in motion and at rest.
Predication	A *one* is the same as itself and the Others, and different from both.
	A *one* is like itself and the Others, and different from both.
	A *one* is equal to itself and the Others, and unequal to both.
Continuum	A *one* touches itself and the Others, and does not touch either.
Conclusion	A *one* is; it is in time; it both is and is not older and younger than itself and the Others; it is of the same age as both; it has a past, present, and future; it can be the object of knowledge, opinion, and sensation.

1. Separateness and Communication Between Oneness and Being

We have seen that pure oneness, as such, cannot exist. So much is this true that, even before we can call it a self-identity, even before a *one* is one, we must associate it to the concept of being. Let us put it this way: being helps oneness to *be* itself; but it is not itself oneness. Oneness will always remain nothing but oneness, and being will always be being. Each of them has an absolute separateness and self-identity.[5] This radical distinction between the two is affirmed many times in the early numbers of the second hypothesis and is only an application of some of the major conclusions of Hypothesis I about the complete separateness from one another of all cosmic factors.

However, if this were all the dialogue would be making no progress at all. The much more important thing to note is that we are still analyzing a *one*, of which oneness and being are now components. For the new supposition is that a *one is*. This oneness is really being taken in two senses: it is an element part, with being, of a whole; and it is also a whole, with these two as structural parts.[6] We are saying, accordingly, much more than that there are both unity and being in the world; we are saying that one communicates with the other, insofar as both co-exist within a whole that is itself

5. 142b 7-8: *ἡ οὐσία τοῦ ἑνὸς ἔιη ἂν οὐ ταὐτὸν οὖσα τῷ ἑνί.* For other passages to the same effect, see *supra*, note 1.

6. 142d 4-6: *Τὸ μὲν ὅλον ἓν ὂν εἶναι αὐτό, τούτου δὲ γίγνεσθαι μόρια τό τε ἓν καὶ τὸ εἶναι.*

again a *one*.[7] Thus the very initial description of this One-Whole already creates a basic antinomy in every entity: each *one* is a whole (which we know to be an absolute indivisible) and each is a many. In a word, two factors are in communion because they exist within the common ambit of some total unity. And this breakdown into antinomical elements is true of any *one*, whether a sensible or a number or a definition or an Idea. As a consequence we are already in the presence of a phenomenon that Socrates has said would fill him with wonder if it were true.[8] He has said that it is easy enough to solve the co-presence of contraries, if such a problem is found only on the level of sensibles; for a sensible particular might participate in the Idea of unity and also in the Idea of plurality and thus, without difficulty, be both one and many.[9] This now turns out to be a superficial solution; for clearly enough, and still from the very analysis of the concept of oneness, the very Idea of oneness, and every Idea (they are all *ones*), is, upon further analysis, a composite of contraries, of one and many.

This would seem, on the face of things, only to intensify the difficulty. Have we done any more than universalize the dilemma? It will be Hypothesis III that will shortly have to bend itself to solving the problem of how a *one* can be many and still remain *one* in the strictest sense. But, fortunately, there are senses in which this very universalizing process will be the means of dissolving important difficulties raised against

7. See 145a, b, c, especially 145c 3. Here, clearly, a *one* is not a part but has parts and beginning and middle and end. See also 145c 4-5, where no doubt is left that it is the *one* that is a whole.

8. 129b 1-2.

9. 129a.

participation. For example, it is true that an indivisible Idea, when it is participated in by such divided phenomena as a man or a beast, becomes dispersed through the parts of these. But if we show that, no matter how many the parts into which *any* entity in *any* order is dispersed, it need not lose the quality of oneness or indivisibility,[10] where is there any sting in the eristic of such objections? Indeed, if the reader is ever on the alert to learn from this *γυμνασία* of the eight hypotheses, he will be picking up all those clues that will enable him to answer the difficulties of the first part of the dialogue; he will also be better able to cope with the whole Aristotelian critique of the Ideas, and he will be ready to handle the attack from the original unpurified Eleatic logic. He will not even be frightened by such an objection as this, that if the transcendent Idea is present in many particulars, it becomes distinct and separated from itself; for he will have learned to search into the sense in which, despite this multiplying and separating presence of an Idea in many sensibles, it remains uniquely one and unseparated from itself. But he will no longer solve such questions after the Eleatic manner by denying the evidence of the senses or refusing to face the facts; rather, he will be equipped both to "save the phenomena" and to save the substantial elements of the Eleatic logic.

10. Notice, for example, how in the *Theaetetus* (205d) Plato treats the concept of a syllable. Though, obviously, it has parts he insists that the syllable itself is *ἀμέριστον*, without parts. And as for the Ideas, no matter how much they seem to be divided by definition, he always refers to them as pure units. See *supra*, pp. 69 ff.

Hypothesis II

A. THE ONE-MANY IS REALLY A LIMIT-UNLIMITED (*142e–144e*)

Plato is concerned to show that there is a much more profound division of any unity than that of unity or oneness on the one hand and a definite and limited number of parts on the other. The concept of oneness is about to be transformed into that of limit, the concept of many numerable parts into that of an unlimited. He does not here indicate the *necessity* of such a transformation, but it is impossible to understand the *Parmenides* unless we begin to recognize that it has a symphonic quality and that each step is preparing for a later important development. Therefore it will be well to pause at this point in order to appreciate the crucial nature of the present passages. The reason for the invention of the notion of the unlimited will only be *perfectly* clear when the eighth hypothesis has been concluded. But enough may be indicated here and now to prepare the reader for the later course of events.

In brief, much of the metaphysics of Plato would be impossible without the notion of the indefinite. It holds a crucial position not only in this dialogue but also in the whole of his later work. If, for example, he should hold to the narrower conception of a *one* as composed of a definite principle of unity and of definitely numerable parts, then he would have created logical and metaphysical problems for himself that are insoluble. I think that this will become clearer when we deal with the content of Hypothesis III. For there the question of the source of the fundamental unity of any complex entity arises for the first time, and if a definite oneness were attempting to unify members that are already definite units in their own right, this would be quite impossible. I merely make the plea that such consequences be held in mind, or else we will be inclined to think that we are, at this moment, witnessing a trivial, though clever, piece of dialectic.

B. THE PROOF FOR THE UNLIMITED

As a matter of fact, the process of establishing the unlimited element in a *one* is entirely dialectical or conceptual. The proof takes three forms: (1) Both elements already discovered in oneness (one and being) are themselves in turn composed of the same factors (one and being); but this division can be extended indefinitely. Hence there is an infinitely divisible principle in oneness. (2) The second proof takes the guise of the generation of an infinite number series. Once again the dialectic depends upon the logic of Hypothesis I. Unity does not differ from being insofar as it is unity, nor being from unity insofar as it is being. The source of the difference lies in *otherness,* which is a factor not identical with either. Granted so much, we can rapidly derive the concepts of "one," of "two," of "three," of "twice," of "thrice," of "twice two," and "thrice three," and so on *ad infinitum.* But each of these numbers is an existent. Therefore, the concept of being (as an original member of the simplest Whole from which we took our start) is multiplied infinitely within that Whole. (3) A similar process of infinite divisibility is executed for the element of oneness.

I am inclined to think that these three processes are not

meant to be proofs in the strict sense at all. Rather, Plato has profound metaphysical reasons for believing in an unlimited element in all being. It is necessary for the solution of certain crucial problems in philosophy. The rather artificial dialectic by which he here establishes it should be taken as a kind of symbolism representing what he means. This infinite division of *concepts* gives some sense of the infinite divisibility resident in the ontological structure of any *entity*.

C. AN UNLIMITED IN EVERY ORDER

Is there an unlimited, a principle of indeterminacy, in every order of being? One has to recognize the difficulties of this question for Platonic scholarship, since it is the focal point of so many Aristotelian remarks on the nature of "later developments" in the theory of Ideas. Aristotle tells us in the *Metaphysics* that for the Academy a limit and unlimited are the elements of all things;[11] that numbers are generated from the *One* and the *indefinite dyad;*[12] that the Ideas are composed of the *One* and the great-and-small.[13] Such views as these, Aristotle tells us, were contained in the "unwritten doctrine" of Plato.[14] These Aristotelian texts — and a host

11. 987b 19.
12. 1080b 14-15.
13. 988a 7 ff.
14. *Physics* 209b 14, 35. Here we find ourselves in the midst of the question of the status of Aristotle's explanation of the Ideas as Idea-numbers derived from two ultimate principles — which principles are somehow the principles of all reality. We are indebted to Cherniss (I, xii-xxi) for his fine critical summary of the more important bibliographical material on this vexing subject. And, for a capitulation of all the Aristotelian texts

of others on the so-called Ideal Number doctrine of later Platonism — have led to a good deal of controversy and confusion, the greater part of which has no relevancy here. The only question of present importance is: was Aristotle right in saying that Plato had universalized the function of limit and unlimited — for Ideas, for numbers, for sensibles, for all things?

---

involved, see the important work of Léon Robin, *La Théorie platonicienne des idées et des nombres d'après Aristote* (Paris: 1908), pp. 267 ff.

To accept our own view of the *Parmenides,* it is not at all necessary to be a devoted follower of Aristotle as an interpreter of Platonism. Indeed, Cherniss (I, xxi) cites Paul Shorey in the latter's review of Stenzel's "*Zahl und Gestalt,*" [*Classical Philology,* XIX (1924), 382] to the effect that "we do not really know what Aristotle's testimony is. . . . It is in particular quite impossible to determine how much of Aristotle's polemic against ideal numbers . . . refers to Plato and how much only to the misunderstandings or developments of Platonism in the Academy."

In general, it is here better to avoid all such questions as these: are all the Ideas numbers and what is the hierarchical placing of Ideas and Idea-numbers? I would myself repeat that Aristotle is right at least in saying that for Plato all reality (if we omit the Good) is composed. But here a word of warning is due. We have no reason to think from the *Parmenides* that the composing principles are existentially or numerically the same in the order of Ideas and becoming. In fact, it is impossible for me to conceive that this is so. Once again our distinction is to be repeated: they are essentially, not numerically, the same. The *Parmenides* waives this whole problem and has nothing to do with the existential question. But we may call upon the whole tone of the dialogues in believing that the Ideas, in their transcendent existence, do not enter into the sensible. That, therefore, would also seem to be true of their indeterminate element (for its various names, see Robin, *op. cit.*, pp. 276 ff., who lists the Dyads of the Great and Small and the Unequal, the Indefinite Dyad, the Multiple, the Different, the Other, the Excess and Defect). There is no evidence from the dialogues that the "material" element of the Ideas is the material element of phenomena. And the *Parmenides* itself does only two things: it fixes the two principles that are structurally and functionally the same in all beings; in subsequent hypotheses it will establish that the same relations exist between these principles as they are found in any order. These relational laws are always identical; the realities that are related are not.

If our reading of the meaning of the hypothesis is correct, there *is* a sense in which he is right. And it is probably unnecessary to go beyond the dialogues themselves to the testimony of Aristotle in order to discover this sense. As Ross[15] indicates, the *Philebus* is of special value on this point. The *Parmenides* itself gives us a philosophy of oneness that is universal in its referability, and here it is proposing the breakdown of all unities, whether ideal or numerical or sensible, into a composition of limit and unlimited. The conclusion is clear. If this is correct, Aristotle is basically right, though it is unwise to follow his testimony in detail. For example, it seems hardly less than absurd to suppose that the principle of indeterminacy is numerically the same for Plato in all the orders of the real. And it seems incorrect to think that the Platonic notion of indeterminacy or unlimitedness ought to be equated with the Aristotelian idea of second matter.[16] If we avoid these two distortions, we shall be on comparatively safe ground in understanding the "later view" of Plato.

For he *would* say generally that there is a dual principle in the structure of all being. One reason why he says it, I have suggested, is that otherwise he cannot solve the metaphysical problem of the unity of a being, but the irritating necessity of solving this problem holds for every level of being. What precisely he can mean by this unlimited principle is another and even more difficult question. On the level of sensibles there can be no misunderstanding, for the notion of the infi-

15. *Op. cit.*, pp. 170-71.
16. Albert Rivaud, *Le Problème du devenir* (Paris: 1906), p. 276: " . . . platonisme est proprement incompréhensible, si l'on veut à tout prix introduire une doctrine de la matière qui ne s'y rencontre pas."

nite divisibility of matter is now, fortunately, a commonplace for our minds. And the infinite fractionization of any number-unit suggests one easy application in that order. But it is in the world of Ideas that our suggestion of the infinite referability of this logic may be controverted most. Yet Plato does seem to be insisting that there is *some* sense in which Ideas or essences themselves are infinitely divisible. Each "part" or phase of an Idea is itself divisible into aspects and this is no mere infinity of logical analysis that bears no relation to the real. Still, I am not proposing that there is an *actual* infinity of "parts" in an essence, for its potential divisibility is always held in check and reduced to definiteness by the limit or one-ness — even in the order of matter. Neither Plato nor Aristotle ever held to an actual infinite of any kind. But, as a general summary of this delicate matter, we might cite the sound statement of Ross[17] who, while accepting the universality of the limit-unlimited in the *Philebus*, has this to add:

"Plato appears to be putting forward a fresh analysis *whose relation to the ideal theory* [italics mine] he has not worked out. But in the description of the unlimited as τό μᾶλλόν τε καὶ ἧττον we cannot fail to see an anticipation of it as τὸ μέγα καὶ μικρόν, and we must suppose that the doctrine of the *Philebus* was the starting-point from which Plato worked in developing the later doctrine."

This discussion can be temporarily closed with the remark that, if Plato actually intended the projection of his limit-unlimited theory of composition into the Ideas, there is, outside of Aristotle, no finer or clearer indication of his meaning

17. *Op. cit.*, p. 171.

than in our current passages and in other later hypotheses of the *Parmenides.*

At any rate, we are now at the point where we have finished our first description of the structure of a *one,* and everything in the hypotheses that follow is but viewed as a consequence of this general structure. The basic truths to be remembered are: any unity is a whole and a set of parts; this may further be refined into a structure of limit-unlimited; the sum of the parts, the many, is the *one;* there is a sense, therefore, in which this sum is both the *one* and not the *one.* Let us now see what consequences develop from this fundamental identity and distinction between the one as unity of wholeness and as many (for everything that ensues depends upon *this* contrariety). Hypothesis I had said that there is a problem field (of selfhood and absolute, unrelated positivity in things) in which all predication and contrariety can validly be denied to a *one* (οὔτε . . . οὔτε); and this denial was meant not as a set of dilemmas but as a positive, ontological description of a principle of being. Hypothesis II now indicates the validity of a καί . . . καί predicability of contraries for a *one.*

2. *Articulation of a* one (*144e-145b*)

It is possible to interpret these lines, with one exception, as applying to all fields of being, to all oneness. In any *one,* its principle of oneness contains and limits all its parts, and it is a many as well as a limiting agent. As a thing of member parts, it is articulated according to a certain ordered jointing and can therefore be said to have a beginning, middle, and end. In the case of a sensible unity, this articulation or structuring of elements will receive the characterization of straight or round or some mixture of the two. Thus the identical unity that in Hypothesis I could not possibly receive any of these qualifications now receives them all. And with the exception noted, of the straight and round, this holds, in some analogous sense at least, for all unities.

3. *The "Place" of a* one (*145b-145e*)

We now begin to ask a long series of questions about any *one*. In what is it, what is its place? Is it in motion or at rest? Is it the same as or different from itself, the same as or different from others? And so with the qualities of likeness and equality. Further, does it have contact with itself, with others? Is it younger or older than, or of the same age as, itself? All these questions can be answered by a double affirmation of contrariety, by a *καί . . . καί* answer. There is a sense in which each contrary affirmation is true. A *one* is in itself and in others, at rest and in motion, and so on.

I believe that the whole structure of a whole series of demonstrations to follow depends on several crucial new findings. The most important of these is that a *one* is both an indivisible whole and a set of parts and *is identical* with itself under this new duality. The second is that these two structural principles, whole and set of parts, *are not identical;* this lack of complete identity between two things that are both the *one* gives ground for a failure of identity between a *one* and itself.

This is a new structure compared to the first hypothesis, where there was no duality in a *one* (no duality of *one* as whole and as parts). It is this new duality that makes it possible for an entity to be in place and motion and rest.

As to place: if *a one* is its parts and is also a whole, and if the parts are in the whole, then *a one* is in itself. Thus far there is no difficulty. But with the second half of the argument I must present alternatives, the first of which seems to fit more strongly into the general dialectic of the hypothesis: (1) If reversely, the whole is not contained within any, some, or all of its parts, then a one is not in itself. This may only mean that a one is not in itself *as a set of parts*. If it is then declared that it is in another, this "other" can be interpreted as the *one* under the second of its dual formalities, the whole. This rendering saves us from going outside of a *one* for an understanding of what "other" means and keeps the whole dialectic of the hypothesis flowing between the internal dual structure of an entity. (2) The alternative is that of Cornford: if the whole is not in the parts, it is in another, and that other is physically other; it is space; this space would be the container of both whole and parts.

It would be an unnecessary limitation to conceive that Plato is merely talking about the problem of *sensible* place when he uses the word "in." Such a mistake would come from the failure to recognize one of the essential points of the whole *Parmenides*, which is that the contrarieties of the sense world can only be understood as a reflection of the contrariety at the core of all being. If there is a sense in which the sensible is both in itself and in another, it is only because the same is true of the transcendent Idea as well.

We may note here too, and with special emphasis, that something else has been accomplished. It is that we have established the possibility of predication. True, the predication is limited, for the moment, to the tautological judgment (*one* is one) that was not yet possible in terms of the first hypothesis. But all other judgments will become possible and valid once this fundamental judgment emerges. And it can now be made because of the discovered difference between a *one* and its *many*. Thus this very judgment of self-identity can only have resulted from the structure established at the core of a *one*. If the *one* were only an absolute, undivided self-identity, no judgment about it would be in order. But it is its parts, yet the two are different. Therefore, in this identity and difference, we have the foundation for judgment, which is basically a statement of identity and difference between terms — a *one* is one.

I say these things in a deliberate approach to Hegelian terms, only to make clear that, as certain surface qualities of the first hypothesis opened the way to innumerable, though unfortunate, Neoplatonic and anti-Eleatic readings, now the present texts have been taken as the favorite ground for some Hegelian readings. Hegel himself had been profoundly influenced by the *Parmenides* and had called it the greatest masterpiece of ancient philosophy. It is not necessary here to indicate anything but a few of the germ ideas he proposed to have discovered in the dialogue: difference as the very soul of identity, negation as the principle of difference, negation as the principle of mediation making possible the return of a thing upon itself in self-identity; only after such a process of differentiation and mediation can we really know a thing; "the perfect immediate is the perfect mediate." This much in general, however, may be said of the relationship between the views of Hegel and of Plato as they are expressed in our dialogue. The aim of both is the same, to construct a general logic of all being, and therefore, in this important sense at least, the Hegelian commentator is on far more solid ground than the Neoplatonist or anti-Eleatic.

4. *Motion and Rest* (*145e-146a*)

But let us continue with this theme of "in itself" and "in another." Now we are told that a *one*, precisely because it is always "in itself," is always at rest; for this is nothing but a definition of rest. And as it is always "in other," it is always in motion. The question arises, as it does in a few other instances: do these passages apply to all the forms of unity in all the orders of the real, including the unchanging Ideas? Or do they constitute one of those recurring parentheses that have exclusive reference to the sensibles, that is, to the order of actual physical motion?

If the first is the case and if the text is universally applicable, then we must understand the application in a somewhat metaphorical sense. Actual motion, according to our formal, mundane meaning of the term, conveys the idea of always being "in other" and always changing into another and another place. Metaphorically, however, Plato would be suggesting that an analogy for this motion is found in the world of the Ideas, because a *one* as a set of parts is always in another, i.e., in a whole which is other than its parts. This is motion in the broadest possible sense, this process of "transition" in locating the identity of a thing now in the *one* as whole and now in its parts, in the one and in its many-others. But as every *one* always remains itself, it is also always at rest.

If we are to make an exclusive application to sensibles, then we have the material here for an explanation of the principle of continuity in actual, formal motion. As Aristotle himself points out,[18] what supplies continuity in local motion is the continuous self-identity of the thing being moved. At any rate, there is a sense in which that which *is* in movement does *not* move; and if this were not so, then it would be impossible to explain *a* movement. For what would make it a unique movement with its own quality and identity? Should this be the present Platonic point — and it is apparently at least one of the points of reference — then we are dealing with the first one of three kinds of continuum problems raised in Hypothesis II: the continua of motion, magnitude, and time. Actually, Plato essays to solve the dilemmas involved in these spatio-temporal problems, but he would not do it unless he had first described the general metaphysical structure of a *one* as limit-unlimited. It is of the nature of every continuum to involve the elements of indivisibility or oneness and of infinite divisibility. Furthermore, we have been given our first sign that the Parmenidean logic still holds over against all divisibility and must enter into the explanation of the very phenomena that it thought it must deny: multiplicity, change, all the forms of continuity. None of these

18. *Physics* 227a 20 ff.; 228b ff.

destroys, none of these can do without, the doctrine of the indivisible, homogeneous, unchanging *one* established in the first hypothesis.

5. *Identity and Difference* (*146a-147b*)

The series of arguments that follows may be summarized thus: we have divided an original indivisible *one* into a structure of unity and of manyness. We have just established that there is a relationship of identity and diversity between these elements. Actually, we may say that the pair "a *one is* its many" and "a *one* is *not* its many" is the first contrariety Plato achieves as a first modification of an over-rigid statement of the principle of contradiction. Now he proceeds to show us that, this much established, we can go on to build up a subordinate series of contrary relations existing between a *one* and its parts or "others." The three pairs of contrary predicates he chooses for this exhibition are sameness-difference, likeness-unlikeness, equality-inequality (though, as in Hypothesis I, he could have extended this series of qualities infinitely). The conclusions he comes to are: (a) a *one* is the same as and different from itself; a *one* is the same as and different from the others; (b) a *one* is like and unlike itself; a *one* is like and unlike the others; (c) a *one* is equal and unequal to itself; a *one* is equal and unequal to the others. (Between [b] and [c] a section on contact and continuum intervenes, but I have so arranged things that the discussion of the above three predicates be unbroken.)

There is little subtlety involved in the first demonstration:

a *one* is not a part of itself taken as a whole; nor is it a whole of which it would itself be a part. Thus we eliminate two conceivable ways in which a *one* can differ from itself. Nor is it *altogether* distinct from itself, i.e., numerically, as whole to whole. Thus we exhaust all the possible ways of being different, so that a *one* must, therefore, be the same as itself. It is as simple a matter to prove that a *one* is different from itself. For all we need do is recur to the dichotomy and identity already created in any entity between its unity and its parts; a one is its parts, but it is also not its parts; therefore not that which is itself.

Again, when we pass on to the relation between a *one* and its others, it is still an easy matter to indicate that there is a relationship of difference between them. The principle of manyness is certainly not the principle of unity in anything. The many as such are not the same as the *one*.

But the last issue involved, the predication of sameness between a *one* and its others (or "parts"), is quite subtle and extremely important. We have just indicated a sense in which unity is different from its members. Now, once again because of the demands of metaphysics and of certain basic problems relating to unity in things and to the requirements of a continuum, we must prove that there is no difference between unity and parts. The very structure of things demands a sense in which the two are different *and not different.* I think the whole matter will be clearer if at this moment we translate the word "difference" by the word "interval" and realize that Plato is denying the existence of any real interval or distance, whether metaphysical or spatial or temporal, between unity and its parts.

This whole problem of the nature of difference will be treated explicitly and at length in Hypothesis V; therefore, it will not here be necessary to give anything but a sketch of the background of the present Platonic argument.

Briefly, difference or otherness is a form of non-being; it is not absolute non-being but is the kind of nothing that is rooted in a positive, limited being and that gives the latter its status as a limited entity that *is not* things other than itself. In order more sharply to clarify the nature of this form of nothingness, let us look at the relationship between two essences that are contraries: equal and unequal. Equality *is not,* is other than, and different from inequality. Now there is no measurable progression from equality to inequality, in the act of transition between the two, for any thing changing from being equal to being unequal; there are no intermediate essences to be crossed before one becomes the other. The distance between the two is not measurable in any such metaphysical terms, or in any other terms. The difference, or interval, is not in either contrary, nor is it in any factor between the two. Thus we can say, not that there is no difference between things, but that the difference between them *is not,* is not measurable or calculable in terms of being.

Actually, this is what Plato is now saying. Only he is applying these propositions to the relation, not between any two essences or contraries, but to that existing between a unity and its members. If there is no measurable interval between such contraries (where one of them is in no sense ever the other), how much more so is this true in the case of the oneness and manyness of an entity (where in one sense a kind of identity can and does exist between the two). Plato is now affirming that yes, there is a sense in which the *one* is not its many parts, but even according to the mode in which this holds, the "interval" differentiating them is not to be reckoned in terms of being.[19] And thus it becomes possible for the careful philosopher to declare, almost in the same breath, at least in contiguous passages, that there is a difference and *is not* a difference between the two basic elements of any entity, any one-many. For difference is not; it is relative non-being.

The next passage (147a-b) advances to the demonstration that not only is the *one* not different from its many; the two are actually the same. This is no mere play on words but involves a real progression. I have just suggested that there is no *positive* difference, no measurable distance in terms of being, between two contraries that pass one into the other. It remains, however, that they are unalterably not the same; one can never become the other. But, we may repeat, the relations of non-difference between two contraries and be-

19. Cornford holds that these texts on the non-difference between *one* and *others* expose the element of conceptual unity or sameness in all the numerically different members of a class. The *others* are thus the other members of one class. It is this, he says, that is meant by the phrase, "difference is never in what is the same" (there can be no class difference in the members of the same class). How he would explain the phrase immediately following ("difference can never be in anything that is") I do not know. The problem has been avoided by omission. I do not see how it can be solved except in the manner above, by remembering the *Sophist's* constant reference to difference as a form of non-being. Cornford seems generally hesitant about finding the conclusions of the *Sophist* in the *Parmenides*. Perhaps it is this hesitancy that forces him into his special reading of Hypothesis V. *Moreover, we are not yet proving that the elements involved are the same, but only that there is no difference between them (such as would involve any kind of positive being in the factor called "difference").*

tween a *one* and its many are altogether different. The two contraries are completely determinate, oppose each other as whole to whole. On the other hand, we have long ago eliminated any possible relationship of a *one* to its members that may be stated in these latter terms; they do not exist externally to each other, but are components of one whole. Even within this unity, however, it is not a case of the *one* relating itself as whole to *definite* parts. For the members of the unity are, of themselves, an infinite or indeterminate and have no status as numerable parts; otherwise they would themselves be "ones." Furthermore, and for the same reason, they are not themselves unities of which the *one* would be a part. In sum, then, we do not have an external relationship of determinate to determinate; nor do we have an internal relationship between two definites. Rather, we have, within the same whole, a determinate over against an indeterminate, between which there is no measurable interval of being. Plato now feels entitled to say that the only alternative left is a declaration of sameness between a *one* and its "others." He will not enlarge on this identity in stricter metaphysical terms until Hypothesis III and Hypothesis VIII. For therein, as already indicated, he will move more decisively toward a clearer declaration: (1) that all the definiteness of the many parts, all their predicability, comes from association with a *one* (III); (2) all their being comes from the same *one* (VIII). It will be in these more precise and profound directions that the one and many will be found to be the same. But the ground for these fuller statements is being laid here.

6. *Likeness and Unlikeness* (*147c-148d*)

The study of the next set of contrary predicates (likeness-unlikeness) will contain sense only if we return to the memory of the original difficulties presented to us by Parmenides in the first half of the dialogue. For example: there we had been told that if a transcendent Idea finds itself present in some way or other in many concrete instances, it is then divided from itself and loses its original unity and purity. True enough, Plato would seem to be saying here in the second half, but we must learn to distinguish a sense in which it is so divided and a sense in which, despite this multiplication, it remains undivided from itself. And so with other problems involving division and dispersion of unities. There will be a mode of existence for any unified fact according to which, despite all division, it remains an absolute indivisible; another according to which it suffers dispersion and manyness. We cannot be trained too carefully in making these distinctions and in understanding these "dilemmas" and their possible solution. The present texts are nothing but somewhat exaggerated examples of this kind of training. They are in no way meant to supply actual answers to our original dilemmas. In fact, they are the only portions of the hypotheses that may be described as predominantly "clever" and somewhat sophistical. Their primary intention is a "training" in the most technical sense of the word. And all they wish to say is that there is a sense in which precisely the common possession of difference makes any two things similar; and a sense in which the common possession of sameness makes them different.

A *one* is different from its others (or parts); this has been clearly established and there is no need of re-establishing it. But, by the same token and by the same difference, the parts of a *one* are different from it. The possession of the identical character of difference makes the two like each other. Is there a sense in which this is perfectly true? There is. Actually, however, Plato could have gone further and could have indicated the extreme difference between the possession of this same character of difference and any other "same" character. For it is true that difference or otherness is an Idea, as much as any other Platonic Idea, but it alone, among all the transcendent forms, has the function of *making to differ* those entities that possess it. He could also have put the matter in another way: the Idea of difference is the same Idea in all the things that are different from one another. But it is also true that each participant in this same Idea, in relation to any other participant, is a *different part* of *difference*. For each entity, difference from other things is exhausted only by the remainder of the universe; but each thing in that remainder is a different part of difference. We might, then, put it this way: A and B both participate in difference, but, in relation to each other, are completely distinct parts of the Idea. I say that Plato does not go on to refine his proposition here because it is only his intention to indicate that there is *some* propriety, no matter how thin, in calling any two things similar by reason of their very diversity. I believe he is saying that, as long as you realize both the identity rooted in difference and the thinness of the same, your dialectical training and ability to solve the difficulties inherent in the theory of Ideas are excellent.

Exactly the same critique can be suggested for the argument that follows. We have proved in our previous inquiries that a *one* is the same as all its parts, or the Others. Now, if difference makes any two things similar, then sameness, which is the contrary of difference, should produce the contrary effect, i.e., difference. Thus, by very virtue of being the same, A and B would be diverse.

I cannot help, then, but think it somewhat unfortunate to say, as Cornford does,[20] that of these two arguments the one is "sound," the other "questionable." Both have precisely the same quality and the same final intent, and it may be repeated that in these places alone does the Plato of the *Parmenides* have his tongue somewhat in his cheek. It seems without point to go any further with these difficult constructions.

7. *Discrete and Continuous* (*148d-149d*)

If we were to define a continuum, it would be best here to do so by summing up its major qualities. I should say, first of all, that a continuum is *one* magnitude that contains in itself a unity of a many and a continuating one. According to Aristotle's doctrine, there are many parts, but these parts have a continuous character by virtue of their boundaries or limits being one and the same. The beginning of one part is the end of the other. Furthermore, these parts are always infinitely divisible. The problem of the nature of a physical

20. *Parmenides*, p. 165.

continuum is, in its own order, only a reflex of the nature of the unity of any entity in any order that is composed of "parts" essentially, numerically, or physically "adjacent" to one another.

If these parts are altogether and unreservedly discrete and are separate units, then unity and continuity are impossible. These members must be not only different but in some way the same as well. It is true that in any such entity there must be a division between its principle of unity and its parts, but there must also be some principle of unity between them, or else once again we run into a pure discrete and no unity at all.

I am about to suggest that in these two different emphases lies the difference between the Aristotelian and Platonic approaches to the nature of a continuum. The former is more engaged with the continuously unified relation of part to part. (This also holds true for the order of essences, where Aristotle conceives that each specifying factor is the actuality of the previous generic factor that is in potency to the new quality. Thus the genus is a subject, whether ontological or logical, for a new development, whether the latter be a species in the real order or a predicate in the logical.) Plato, on the other hand, is preoccupied with the relation of the total unity to the total parts of a thing, and he conceives that the source both of the discreteness and the unity of the parts in their successive relation to each other is not from themselves but from the total unity or the *one*. All of this he will say quite explicitly in Hypothesis III. But it will be interesting to see how even now, in the following Platonic comments on the nature of unity and the continuous, he is again laying the groundwork for what is to come. The development is the usual one: there is a contrariety of touching and not-touching between the elements of a *one*. Where there is "touching" it is meant that there is some measure of discreteness between two touching things; where there is "not-touching" it is meant that the two things are really one indivisible.

There is some degree of discreteness between a *one* and its parts, between a *one* and itself. This is only to say again, though now in terms of a new problem, that we have succeeded in breaking down the original complete indivisibility of a *one* and discovering two principles that are both different and identical: a *one* and its parts. Since they *are* different, one principle can be in the other and "touch" it. But since one and parts are also the same, then the touching and discreteness that has been established is between the *one* and itself.

On the other hand, if we also remain faithful to the constantly fundamental premise of Hypothesis I, a *one* always retains its principle of absolute oneness and indivisibility, despite all dispersion into parts. It is this factor that Plato fastens upon as the principle of continuity that keeps a thing *a* thing. For such continuity there must be an element in which discreteness is altogether impossible. Thus, Plato never discusses the Aristotelian problem of the unity that is effected in a spatial reality by virtue of the possession of identical limits in consecutive parts. His "physics" of continuity — indeed, as we shall see later, his whole logic — tends rather in the direction already described.

Now, however, we return to a clarification of the discrete relationship between a *one* and its parts. He has already indicated that they are two discrete things. Certainly this must be severely modified, as we have already had to modify our statement of the relationship of *difference* between a *one* as indivisible whole and its parts. Not being one in any sense, the parts are completely indeterminate, they are an infinite; it is, therefore, impossible that they stand over against oneness as a determinate to a determinate. Yet only between such is there true "touching" and true discreteness. Whatever determination the many have — such as would make formal discreteness possible — comes from the *one* itself (read Hypothesis III). And it is necessary for the unlimited parts first to be associated with this total oneness before they can emerge into any kind of discrete relationship even among themselves. We also have the basis here for the further quality of infinite divisibility in the continuum.

8. Equality and Inequality
(*149d-151e*)

The general point being raised in the brief but symbolic array of predicates and their contraries (same-other, like-unlike, equal-unequal) is that a whole series (potentially infinite) of predicates and their contraries, can characterize any *one*. This is the general issue, and it would have been possible for Plato to give substantially the same dialectical proof for the compossibility of all contrary pairs. If, however, he is constantly shifting the nature of his proofs, the explanation is simple. *He is taking individual predicates as pretexts to introduce other subsidiary metaphysical and physical problems.* In what follows, for example, he is not only fortifying his general conclusion with another case of the cohabitation of contraries; he is here also taking the occasion to analyze the nature of relation, or relative being. The reader will have noticed how other problems have been introduced before in the same occasional manner: a metaphysical analysis of *difference* has already been given by way of anticipating a fuller development of this phenomenon in Hypothesis V. Motion and the spatial continuum have come in for illumination in other passages. I am now suggesting that Plato — about to discuss equality and inequality — sees an opportunity to talk about relative being, and it is this that influences the mode of the dialectical argument. He might have chosen a dozen other forms of argumentation, but that would not have served his subordinate goal. Let us see if this is true.

Why is any *one,* any thing, equal to itself? A simple form of dialectic might have said that since a *one* is established long ago as being the same with itself, it is, therefore, equal to itself. The argument, on the contrary, is as follows:

It is true, we are told, that Greatness and Smallness exist; but if they exist as containing, or as dispersed through, or as coextensive with a *one,* then all sorts of impossible consequences develop. Smallness will become Greatness or Equality, and similar absurd consequences will hold for Greatness. The basic error in all these conceptions (of containing, dispersion, coextension) is that such Ideas as Smallness and Greatness are not fully positive entities that are present *in* the reality of a *one.* In this sense, Greatness and Smallness do not exist at all. They are purely relative terms and have only the existence that a relation has. Indeed, the argument is very much like that we have used in the case of the notion of *difference.* Difference is *a* form of relative non-being, a sort of non-measurable interval between A and B. Since it is not *in* either of them as a positive and absolute reality, it was argued that in this sense we cannot say there *is* difference between different things; hence, by virtue of being different, there is no difference between A and B. Apply this kind of subtlety to the present case and the results become intelligible. A relationship is a sort of ratio (λόγος) between two things and cannot be represented by the kind of positive statements we have ascribed to the absolute positivity of A or B in Hypothesis I. In this sense neither Smallness nor Greatness *is*. But if, then, a *one* is in possession of neither Smallness nor Greatness, Plato feels that he is so placed dialectically that he can choose the only remaining alternative: a *one* is *equal* to the others and to itself. All this has nothing at all to do with a rejection of the *Phaedo* doctrine of the presence of Forms in a thing — as Cornford suggests it does.[21] It merely qualifies the assertion of that dialogue about "presence" and participation in such a way as to indicate the unique way in which relational terms are present.

It may be retorted that Equality is also a relative term and hence should be as rigidly excluded from A and B as have Smallness and Greatness. To this there may be either one of two replies: (1) Plato simply does not choose to indicate this as true and leaves its validity to be grasped by the insight of the reader. (2) But he has already given more than sufficient ground for the possibility of *some* predicative relationship between a *one* and itself, between a *one* and its members; hence, if he has eliminated one contrary (Inequality or Greatness-Smallness), he feels it is right and necessary

21. *Op. cit.*, pp. 172-73, 175.

to affirm the other — Equality. Moreover, Equality, strictly speaking, is not a relation at all. Smallness-Greatness involve each other as correlative terms. Equality has no such correlative. In this case correlation only exists between two instances of equality, A and B, which participate in the identical Idea of Equality.[22]

Is there a sense in which a *one* is unequal to itself? Yes, for we have previously indicated that a *one* is *in itself* and a container-contained relation involves the corresponding status of Greater-Smaller. The final question would be, is a *one* unequal to the others, i.e., to its parts? Yes, for in any one thing there is only the *one* and its members. These, however, must in each case be somewhere, be *in* something. As they can only be in each other, we have the identical phenomenon of container-contained and the identical issue of inequality.

This is, perhaps, as good a place as any other to clarify the degree of validity and seriousness that Plato attaches to his proofs for the predicability of contraries. Does he really mean, for example, that the *one* is greater than the *one?* He means it according to the measure and sense and validity of the argument used to establish it. Here, in the sense and to the degree that a *one* as parts is in a whole, it is exceeded by this whole. And so with previous instances of predication. Is there really no difference between two different elements? There is not, in the sense and to the degree that difference has no real positive existence. Is there no relation of inequality between elements? None, in the sense and to the degree that neither does such a relation have an existence of absolute

22. In this I am indebted to the excellent distinction of Cherniss (I, 284-85), who in turn finds the point in Proclus.

positivity. Therefore, in each case the proposition being affirmed or denied must take its qualified meaning from the type of dialectical proof that accompanies it.

9. *Older, Younger, of the Same Age*

A. AS ITSELF (*151e–152c*)

In meaning and importance this section corresponds to the previous analysis of the nature of the spatial continuum; it is nothing more nor less than a series of propositions outlining the structure of the temporal continuum. Time also involves both multiplicity and unity, discreteness and continuity; its very nature is a passage of the *same* thing through *different*, consecutive states. Therefore, as with the problem of spatial magnitudes, it includes a contrariety at the very heart of it.

Once again let us suppose our original successful dichotomizing of a *one* at the beginning of Hypothesis II. What form does this dichotomy take in the phenomenon of a *one* that is subject to time? Surely it passes through successive times and yet, in some necessary sense, the *one* of a later moment is the *one* of a previous. Thus the *one* of the earlier moment is becoming older than the *one* of a later; the *one* of the later moment is becoming and is younger than itself as constituted in the earlier. Therefore, we may say that the *one* is both older and younger than itself. But, seeing that a *one* (here, as ever, we fall back on Hypothesis I) is perpetually itself, present to itself, and never departing from self, it is always of the same age as itself. Even the variegated processes of "a time," the life-history of a *one*, connotes the retention of the Parmenidean doctrine of absolute unity and indivisibility over against every appearance to the contrary. Thus, time and history are not a series of isolated and distinct appearances or creations, as Descartes will later propose. It is, rather, a veritable continuity. And it cannot be repeated too often that this particular pole of the contrariety in time, as in the case of every contrariety we have thus far discovered, depends totally on the very first step achieved in the eight hypotheses, depends completely on Parmenides. Plato's real achievement is to harmonize the Eleatic philosophy with the evidence of the senses and history.

B. AS THE OTHERS
(*152e-155d*)

To understand the ensuing argument, it is necessary to clarify the meaning of the terms "one" and "others." Here, for the first time in the dialogue, the word "one" has a number of different meanings and the dialectic depends on the constant disentangling of these. Cornford would have it that the successful penetration into the meaning of the hypotheses involves the constantly shifting sense in the two basic terms — of *one* and *others* — but there is no other example of such tortuous twisting; and even here the very metaphysical problem involved includes, of its very nature, many meanings for *unity*. Two are outstanding: (a) Time means the passage of an abiding *one* through historical stages. This *one* is the spatially or metaphysically constituted unity we have already studied. (b) But a series of "chronic" intervals making up a time is also a *one*, is *a time*, and is the actual temporal unity or continuum that we are now dissecting. Thus, to put the two meanings together, we may say that the *one* passes through a *one* which is *a time*. Furthermore, (c) the first moment of this time is a *one* — it is the *one* having one moment of time — the others are its later stages. (d) The last moment is that in which the one total time stands completed as a temporal unity; the "others" are then understood as all the previous stages. (e) Finally, the *one* is constantly and completely present through all these stages. (Aristotle might say that each "now" is perpetually different but is also the same by virtue of the constant identity of the subject passing through every "now".) Holding in mind all these meanings for unity in the temporal continuum, we shall derive the sense of the following Platonic propositions:

1. The first moment of a time — call it the *one* (c) — is older than the others considered as the total stages of the time series. 2. The last moment of a time is that in which *a one time* (b) is completed — and this *one,* coming into completed being only at the end, is, therefore, younger than the others, or all the previous stages. 3. But the *one* (a) is constantly present to the totality of these time developments that we call the *others* and is, therefore, of the same age as they. Again, then, this abiding self-identity (a) is the root cause of the continuity of the whole time series (b). Thus the paradox: if it is true, from the first hypothesis, that there can be no question of spatial or temporal quality in the simple character of a *one* as there described, it is equally true that the spatial or temporal continuum cannot exist without such complete indivisibility and self-identity. Now, however, with the combination of the two elements, the indivisible and the

infinitely divisible, the *one* and many, the discrete and continuous, we recognize our world of reality and the whole of it becomes possible. It has always been actual to our eyes; now it is *logically* possible. There is an order of time, of past, present, and future; therefore, there is also an order of becoming.

And what is more, all the types of knowledge that are properly human are now supplied with their proper objects. A pure *one* is, in the technical sense, unknowable, but not so with a Whole that is a combination of unity and multiplicity. Knowledge is always knowledge of a one-many; it recognizes the many elements as one and a *one* as a dispersed and divided fact. It is thus that we know essences and definitions and numbers and even the one-many realities of sense, the spatial magnitude, and all forms of the continuum.

6

HYPOTHESIS II A

The Problems:

The subject is the nature of the interval (or instant) in the time process. The relation between contraries as they exist, not co-instantaneously, but in successive moments of time. Coming to be (a passage from non-being to being); passing-away (being to non-being); combination (many to one); separation (one to many); alteration (change in quality); increase and decrease (change in quantity); locomotion (rest to motion, motion to rest).

The instant of change or passage is not measurable, and cannot receive the name of positive being. In the instant, a *one* cannot receive the predication of either of the two contraries involved (e.g., at the moment of change to motion, a thing is neither in motion nor at rest). The interval, therefore, is another of the positive forms of non-being. A comparison between difference, relation, and this interval.

We now have a thoroughgoing one-many on our hands. How shall we succeed in returning to the rigorous unity of Hypothesis I?

6

It should now be clear that it is the intention of the eight hypotheses to discuss as many problems in the logic, the metaphysics, and the physics of the Platonic system as is possible in their brief compass. The over-all question that receives most attention, at least on the dramatic surface of the second half of the dialogue, is that of the predication of contraries. And the laws of this predication, we have said, shift according to the nature of the phenomenon being studied. We have discovered why it was impossible to ascribe either of two contraries to the phenomenon of unity as such in the opening hypothesis. We have, in the second, likewise discovered the validity of the application of both contraries to the general phenomenon of a whole which is a one-many and to all the subordinate phenomena discussed within such a new world. Now, in the appendix that is added to this section (it is traditionally called II A), the external form of predication suddenly and briefly returns to the original form of the first hypothesis: that is to say, we again deny that either of two contraries can be applied to a *one*. But we have by this time acquired the dialectical habit of being on guard for the emergence of a new question that will call for a new logic of predicates. This appendix, then, does not in any way cancel out any previous series of propositions. It simply recognizes that it has left something undiscussed and proceeds to discuss it. What, therefore, is the new subject?

It is the nature of the *interval*, or *point of transition*, that separates two contraries in the time process of passage from one to the other.

First of all, let us note that there are two basic types of contrariety that are analyzed in this second hypothesis: (1) Within the main body of the hypothesis we have already studied all those forms that may loosely be described as "static." That is to say, these are contrarieties that can exist in a given entity at the same moment and serve as a description of its co-instantaneous structure. Thus, a being is at one and the same moment — though not in one and the same sense — like and unlike, equal and unequal, in motion and at rest, discrete and continuous. This co-instantaneous type of contrariety applies even to the passage of "a time" or period in the history of a *one*, insofar as that time is looked upon itself as a total, self-enclosed unity which can, as one whole, be both one and many, discrete and continuous. (2) The second type, now to be examined in this appendix, involves the relationship between contraries that exist only in successive moments of time. In the first type we are interested in the phenomena of the compossibility at one time of all the forms of being and non-being (e.g., a *one is* and *is not* one). In the second, we concern ourselves with the actual temporal passage of being to non-being or of non-being to being (e.g., a *one* becomes many: disaggregation; or one color becomes another: alteration).[1]

1. 156a, b.

In a word, we are here examining all the types of becoming, under the form of the passage of one opposite to another. These opposites include the following: all coming-to-be, or passage from non-being to being; all "passing-away," or passage from being to non-being; all coming-to-be-one (combination) and coming-to-be-many (separation); all change in quality (alteration) and quantity (increase and decrease); all passage from rest to motion and motion to rest (locomotion).

At least one commentary[2] has gone so far as to say that the two types of contrariety, successive and static, stand to each other in a relation of modification and correction one of the other. According to this view the body of Hypothesis II has ended in a complete ἀπορία: for it is impossible that a *one* at one moment receive a predication of contraries. Such predication can only be applied in successive moments of time in the history of a *one*. Therefore, it is only in the order of time and becoming, as developed in this present appendix, that such antinomies are reconciled. It is as though, in Hegelian fashion, the contradictions in the logic of predication between the first and second hypotheses can only be synthesized in a successive world of process. But all this is certainly not the case, for in the case of each antinomy we have come upon the laborious sense in which contrary predicates are compossible. Rather, all is said when we simply repeat that another type of relation between opposites now emerges for analysis. At this juncture, I should like to point out that the same relation between the body of an hypothesis and the appendix thereto holds for Hypothesis V. There we shall first analyze the co-instantaneous presence of being and non-being (in the

2. See chap. 9, n. 27.

form of otherness or difference) in a *one;* then in an appendix we will be engaged in treating the appearances of being and non-being in a *one* that is "changing." The structural correspondence is perfect, although, as we shall see, the problems are somewhat different.

Then what does Plato say of the succession of contraries? First of all, it is certain that if a thing is now at rest, now in motion, it cannot be so without changing.[3] The same is true for all the other types of transition we have enumerated. "When" does the change occur? I put the word in quotes because the upshot of the matter will be that this "when" is hardly a point of time at all and hardly deserves the name of being. There is no measurable time when a *one* undergoing such change is not either in motion or at rest.[4] Yet the passage is an actual temporal phenomenon. We can only say that there is a point of time outside of time, as it were, which we may call the *instant*,[5] which is the point of transition from A to B and in which a *one* is neither A nor B. There it is neither moving nor resting,[6] if these are the contraries involved; neither like nor unlike[7] (if a *one* is becoming unlike what it was); neither is nor is not[8] (if it is passing away or coming to be); and so with all the forms of change between contraries.

In sum we may reason that the very nature of becoming and time involves some kind of entity not measurable in terms of being, some point of time not measurable in terms of time, at which it is impossible to predicate of a changing

3. 156c 3-5.
4. 156c 6-7.
5. 156d 3.
6. 156e 6-7.
7. 157a 8.
8. 157a 2-3.

thing either one of two involved contraries. There is no calculable transition between being and non-being, for there is nothing between them. Parmenides himself had said that there is being that is and non-being that is not and there is nothing between in this dichotomy. Plato's method of handling the dichotomy is far more subtle; for this *instant* is only the most recent in a series of "intervals" that he has discovered between being and non-being; they exist, each one of them, but cannot be expressed in terms of the positive being of Hypothesis I. Change is indeed real, but it cannot be explained in terms of such a positive real as that of the first hypothesis. It is, however, explained in terms of a positive form of non-being.

Thus, if over against the full positivity and absoluteness of a *one* as described in the opening hypothesis, we summarize some of the results of the second, we see that we now possess no less than three new varieties of being that are altogether different in quality: (1) Difference, or otherness, is a purely relative entity of a negative character; it is a mixture of being and non-being by which the positive *one* enters into a negative relationship with everything other than itself. Hypothesis V will analyze the concept in a more elaborate way; so too, of course, will the *Sophist.* (2) Relational being, such as Smallness and Greatness, involves a real and positive relation to other things; yet it is itself not the positive being of either of two correlates. (3) The interval between two contraries in transition is again real but not positive.

Note the difference in the logic of predication used in these three. Of both types of relative being, negative and positive, the two contraries, being and non-being, may be predicates. Of the *instant* neither may. In this respect the latter is identical with the *one* of Hypothesis I. Yet, despite the identical surface dialectic of these two cases, the ontological implications could not be more diverse than they are. In Hypothesis I, the denial of the possibility of predication, the refusal to identify a *one* with any character, is simply a statement of self-identity and of an as yet unrelated fullness of being with itself. In II A, the meaning of the denial of the predication of either of a pair of contraries to the *instant* is that in this case being is mysteriously and transitionally suspended between two such self-identities and is neither of them.

Before we turn to Hypothesis III, let us locate our present position. Not every problem has been solved in the total second hypothesis by any means. Principal, perhaps, among those that are unsolved is the matter of unity in any true entity. Indeed, while this whole section has clarified many original dilemmas, it has in a sense created one that is more serious than any it has elucidated. For, where we began with an absolute indivisible in Hypothesis I, now we have on our hands a *one* that has at its structural heart a basic dichotomy of elements wherever we turn. It is necessary, then, to retrace our steps, as it were, and, while preserving the whole achievement of Hypothesis II, recover, to the degree that is possible, that unity which makes a thing really one. This calls for nothing less than the study we have promised of the relations between the principle of unity and the principle of manyness in an entity. How far can we go in recovering the happy status, so far as oneness is concerned, of Hypothesis I?

Hypothesis II A

Are the one and the many, limit and unlimited, two things in reality or are they one? Some hints toward an answer have already been indicated; but the question begins to be asked and answered in a highly formal way in the third hypothesis. We now turn to it.

7

HYPOTHESIS III

The Problems:

Where Hypothesis I was the hypothesis of unity, this is the hypothesis of unification. How can the one-many really be one thing? A number seems to be composed of units; how can it be one? So with a definition, whose unit-parts become clear in diæresis.

Aristotle asks the question: how can the Platonic Idea be one? If a thing is only a sheer multitude of units, how account for its precise, ordered structure? The principle of unity is not a "pure third." Not a bond. Aristotle's solution.

For Plato, the many are not a multitude of units. The self-identity, limit, the precise relation to the other parts of everything in the many comes from the one. There is no form in the many that is not received from the one, or is not the one. The doctrine of participation. This doctrine corrects the fallacy of conceiving two beings in a thing, a one and a many, as existing on the same level. How the one prevents the actualizing of infinite division in the indeterminate many. Plato's theory of unity is not the genus-species theory of Aristotle.

7

It may be repeated at this stage that each of the hypotheses implicitly deals in a fairly complete though summary way with some aspect of the doctrine of Ideas. The third hypothesis will prove to be a happy example of this fundamental fact. In contrast with the more complicated framework of the two previous sections, it deals with a single one of those aspects or problems in a highly concentrated way.

In brief, I take Hypothesis III as a study of the problem of the unity of any true entity or fact (or Whole) as it is found in any order of the real. It is, in a special though induced way, an analysis of the unity of any complex Idea.

The second hypothesis has indicated that any unit fact is a whole of parts. We may vary the terms describing the elements of such a unity. They may be conceived of as a whole and its parts; or as a one and a many; or as a limit and an unlimited; or as a sensible body and all its material parts; or as a concept including many member concepts; or as a transcendent Idea composed in some way of many subordinate Ideas. It may also be added — for the logic of the hypothesis also has application here — that the question of the unity of the Ideal Numbers of Plato will also fall within the range of this "representative logic." The Ideal Number "five," for example, is a factor that seems to involve five actual units, and we may very well ask, as in all the other cases, what is there about it, *if anything*, that makes this number one fact.[1] All these things, therefore, are examples of the range of our two basic terms, the One and the Others. In every case, be it noted, these two elements are always contained within the ambit of an "individual" or "Whole," and the crux of the present hypothesis is: how can such a reality be a true individual? If many things exist within the same fact, how can it be One?

The Problems in Plato

Advancing into more properly Platonic territory, we see that, especially in the later metaphysical dialogues, Plato teaches us his own method of breaking down a concept into the whole ordered series of its member units. This process is called diæresis, or division.[2] Generally speaking, it is a method of analysis of concepts that, beginning from the highest genus, dichotomizes the genus into two exclusive divisions and thereafter proceeds, by similar successive dichotomies on one side of this "cutting," to a point where an ultimate specific differentia is reached. If we add the total results in the right-hand column, we have a picture of the detailed internal structure of an Idea or definition. Ignoring for the moment

1. This question is asked a number of times by Aristotle. See, for example, *Metaphysics* 992a 2-3.

2. For a brief summary of the nature of Platonic diæresis, see Cornford's *Plato's Theory of Knowledge* (London: 1935), pp. 184 ff. A detailed analysis of Aristotle's criticism of this logical instrument may be found in Cherniss, I, chap. 1 ("Diæresis, Definition and Demonstration").

all the earlier hints at and analogues of this method, we are given a profusion of examples in the *Sophist* and *Politicus*. Most of these are not to be taken seriously but are only methodological examples. What remains quite clear, nevertheless, is that Plato is convinced that all such divisions into separate units reveal the inner divided nature of things.[3] Again we may ask, what makes a collection of such things *one?* Indeed, Plato himself is quite conscious of the difficulty and he refers in the *Philebus*[4] to the furor aroused by the new method of division — such a furor that the whole original doctrine of indivisible Ideas was being questioned in many quarters.

A whole series of Platonic terms introduces the same problem in one way or other (many of these have already been cited). For example, there is a notion that runs consistently through the dialogues, that of "relatedness."[5] It is true that every cosmic factor is distinct and self-identical — but it is also related in a negative or positive way with every other such factor. It can either fuse or not fuse with every other being. Now, if between any two concepts there is such a positive relationship, then there is a weaving together, a συμπλοκή. If in any way they are compatible, they participate one in the other (μετέχειν). There is between them a communion, a κοινωνία.[6] But this relatedness and these terms do not actually

3. Cherniss holds the contrary, but it is difficult to understand his position (I, 46-47).

4. 15a, b.

5. See the chapter on "relatedness" in Demos, *The Philosophy of Plato* (New York: 1939), pp. 167-73.

6. Diès in his *La Définition de l'être et la nature des idées dans le Sophiste de Platon* cites many kindred terms: προσάπτειν, συναγαγεῖν,

introduce a difficulty distinct from our earlier one. For all such terms either mean that things that are thus fused are really being described as things that can exist together within the same individual; or they fall under some relation — which relation may be considered as a higher, unifying fact containing such members. Again the question: if these self-identical facts are true units, is there — can there be — a true unity which embraces them? If so, how shall we describe it?

Here is the way Aristotle[7] puts the matter against Plato. He asks the question about both definitions and numbers: what is the cause of their being one? If man is really composed of two Ideas such as "animal" and "two-footed," what makes man one? Do not individual men really participate in these two units, rather than in one? Aristotle charges that the doctrine of the Ideas, in the face of such a dilemma, proposes as solution nothing but sheer metaphor and such words as "participation" must be considered as no more than that.[8]

Still a second phase of the dilemma of unity should be covered in this outline of the background of the central problem of Hypothesis III. It may be summarized as the relationship, not of the parts to any dominant (but questionable) unity, but of part to part. Actually the result of diæresis, which is the great tool of Platonic dialectic, is not merely to break down an entity into its members, but to *articulate* it as accurately as possible, to give us a picture of its *jointings*, of the manner in which it is structured in a part-to-part relation-

---

ἀναρμόστεῖν, συναρμόττειν, συνφωνεῖν, ἐπικοινωνεῖν, ἐπιγίγνεσθαι, μεικτόν, σύμμειξις (p. 119).

7. *Metaphysics* 1045a 17 ff.

8. *Ibid.*, 987b 12; 1045b 8.

ship. Thus, we have already come across the words ἄρθρα and μέλη, joints and limbs.[9] The knife of the dialectician must follow the anatomy of nature. The elements of anything are not in *any* kind of juxtaposition, but the relation of each to any other is highly specific. This obvious fact is in constant use in the philosophy of Plato, who draws heavily, for one thing, upon its ethical conclusions. Thus, the final definition of the Good in the *Republic* is τὸ τὰ αὑτοῦ πράττειν;[10] a thing is good when everything in it is in its place and performs its own proper function. Thus, too, in the same dialogue, when Plato is asked how possibly the guardians of the state will consent to be subservient, he answers that their happiness consists in playing the role or part that is theirs by nature and that belongs to no other.[11]

But if this kind of articulation or jointing in things is clear, the resolution of the metaphysical difficulty that lies under it is much less so. For if each part is a real unity, then it is not easy to see why each should "sacrifice" itself to the others by accepting its position. And this holds true whether we are dealing with purely material or biological or moral ordering. Articulation becomes an impossibility in a sheer multitude of unit-parts. Some indivisible principle of unity, some superior principle of articulation, is, then, the only thing that can account for order.

In sum, therefore, the questions to which we must find answers are: how can anything that is composed of parts be one? If the parts are independent units, how can they form a unity?

9. See *supra*, p. 69.
10. 433b.
11. 420d.

Again, if they are units, how can they be *articulated* into a structural unit?

A Solution to Be Avoided

These are the questions. But before we search with Plato for a solution, let us warn ourselves of one direction in which we will find none. We must not look for a point of unity between any two parts or elements in what we may call a "pure third." Any third element that would intervene as a unifying factor cannot help finally taking the form of a pure invasion from the outside. This would be to unite things by a *σύνδεσμος*,[12] by a bond or chain, and would at best be a mechanical process incapable of effecting a real unity. It is pretty plainly this that Aristotle conceives Plato to have done in trying to solve what is for Aristotle a fundamental impossibility at the heart of the Idea doctrine.[13]

To understand this it will be necessary to give a brief résumé of the Aristotelian answer to the dilemma of unity. It is, in a sense, a solution that solves by avoiding the difficulty that would create the problem in the first place. It is not an over-simplification to say that Aristotle sees any two things become one only by their never having been two. He seems to suggest that it is absurd even to ask the question why anything is one.[14] How else can they be one save by being one and the same thing?[15]

12. *Metaphysics* 1045b 13.
13. *Ibid.*, 1045a 16.
14. *Ibid.*, 1045b 19. Cf. Ross, *Aristotle's Metaphysics, in loc.*
15. *Metaphysics* 1045b 18.

For him the two basic elements in a substance — or definition of a substance — are its matter and its form. The matter of a statue is the determinable bronze; the form is the actual figure it finally receives. The matter of a definition is its genus; the form is its final differentia.[16] Now these two, matter and form, are actually one and the same reality, the one being in potency precisely the same thing that the other is in actuality.[17] Thus it is not necessary in his scheme of things to ask what unites the concepts "animal" and "two-footed." "Animal" is (but potentially) "two-footed"; "two-footed" *is* (actually) "animal."

There is no need here to explain the very real dilemmas that are created by Aristotle's own system. For the only point in introducing it at all is to agree with one of its fundamental convictions: that no third supervening or binding element will ever give us a satisfactory metaphysics of being or unity. He is, therefore, perfectly right in protesting against the "bond" of Lycophron and such attempts at solution as are indicated in words like "composition" or "synthesis" — for "the absurdity lies in the application of terms like *σύνθεσις* to things that never existed apart."[18] His criticism of the Ideal Numbers of Plato takes the same turn, for Aristotle cannot conceive how the units he supposes to be in each can become one number "by contact, mixture or mere position."[19]

16. *Ibid.*, 1038a 19-20.

17. *Ibid.*, 1045a 23 ff., b 17-21 (*ἔστι δ', ὥσπερ ἔιρηται, ἡ ἐσχάτη ὕλη καὶ ἡ μορφὴ ταὐτὸ καὶ ἕν, δυνάμει, τὸ δὲ ἐνεργείᾳ*). On the problem of Aristotelian unity, cf. Félix Ravaisson, *Essai sur la Métaphysique d'Aristote*, I (Paris: 1837), 396 ff.; Charles Werner, *Aristote et l'idéalisme platonicien* (Paris: 1910), pp. 41 ff.

18. See Ross, *op. cit.*, on *Metaphysics* 1045b 12-16.

19. *Metaphysics* 1082a 20-21.

Unity in Plato

To begin with the briefest kind of exposition of the content of Hypothesis III, it takes the form of two parts that on first sight constitute a startling paradox.

The first part is given and concluded in a few opening sentences, and its whole point is to say that the *one* is not the *others*.[20] The principle of unity in any fact is not the elements of that fact. This is no more than a repetition of the achievement or discovery of Hypothesis I, that a *one* is identical only with itself. But the principal function of the repetition here is perhaps to indicate Plato's perfect willingness to face the very real problem that the *others* are not the *one*, that there is real multiplicity within things or concepts, and our task is to discover how, despite this, they really remain one.

In the second part, which runs through the remainder of the hypothesis, it develops that a *one* is in a very important sense not distinct from the *others;* the principle of unity is not distinct from its parts. If this is true, if they are really one and the same thing, then the dilemma is avoided. The answer is not that of Aristotle but there is the possibility that it is even more profound and more consistent than his.

For Plato there are many definite and highly specific units in any whole:

> For if each is a part, then the meaning of "each" is surely that it too is one, separated from the other parts and with its own separate existence — if the word "each" is used correctly of it.[21]

20. 157b.
21. 158a.

Now the same thing can be said of the whole or totality of parts. For it too has a recognizable and identifiable character. It is no mere multitude but forms a definite pattern, or εἶδος, and may receive the predicate of unity, though it is not identifiable with oneness. This is the second kind of specificity we can discover in any individual:

> For the part is not part of the many, nor part of all the parts, but rather of some kind of single entity and unity which we call a whole.[22]

Finally, there is still a third type, for not only is there specificity and self-identity in the whole and in the parts but also in the mutual structural relationship of part to part:

> When each part becomes one part, then all have a limit in relation to one another and to the whole, and so with the whole in relation to the parts.[23]

But if for Plato there are all these units and specificities to be discovered in being, there is only one source for all of them and that source is the all-embracing *one*, or principle of unity. Every subordinate and member predicate acquires its definiteness and definability and specificity from this *one*. We do not say here that it also receives its ontological status of very being from the same source, for this more thoroughgoing conclusion will be reserved for the final hypothesis (VIII). For the purposes of the present hypothesis, we are to conceive that, even apart from the *one*, the Others have of themselves *some* real status. Thus separated, they form an

22. 157d-e 1.
23. 158c 7-d 2.

indefinite multitude, though not in the sense that they form a multitude of units, for each member of this mass is an indefinite multitude.[24] We shall say, therefore, that at present they seem to have an internal existence but no internal capacity for predicability.

It is only by their association with the *one*, or unifying principle, that any kind of *identifiable* reality begins to appear. Then only do three things emerge: first of all, a character in each unit emerges (ἕτερόν τι γίγνεσθαι ἐν ἑαυτοῖς);[25] an order which articulates the parts in relation to each other appears (ὃ δή πέρας παρέσχε πρὸς ἄλληλα);[26] and both the whole and the part become identifiable entities (μετέχειν δέ γε τοῦ ἑνὸς ἀνάγκη τῷ τε ὅλῳ καὶ τῷ μορίῳ).[27] All this happens through the activity of the *one* (ἐκ μὲν τοῦ ἑνὸς καὶ ἐξ ἑαυτῶν κοινωνησάντων).[28]

It is, then, not quite accurate to conceive that there is a principle that, proceeding downward, as it were, penetrates each one of the members with definiteness and that, thereafter, these newly constituted unit parts independently relate themselves to one another on the horizontal plane. This second alternative seems to be implied by the idea of communion, or κοινωνία, and all its related phrases. It is true that the members of a whole are now compatible, can exist within a certain individual and according to a certain jointing, but this too is the gift of the *one*, and the *whole* process of making the parts definite and related must be considered as vertical, as proceeding from the formal causality of the *one*. Accordingly,

24. 158c 2-7.
25. 158d 4-5.
26. 158d 5.
27. 158a 6-7.
28. 158d 3-4.

such a criticism as that of Cherniss is correct when he alleges[29] that Aristotle reviewed the whole doctrine of the Ideas in the light of his own theory of genus and species, substance and attribute, matter and form. For Aristotle, the second element of each of these pairs is derivative from, and dependent on, the first. But such a structural picture does not accurately portray Plato's concept of unity, as is clear from the above.

At the end of things, therefore, it is revealed that there is no form of the definite that is not in the *one*, that is not the *one*. It pervades all and determines all. This is true if we look first at the unity of all the parts as a whole. How now does this unity differ from the *one?* How, that is to say, does the sum of the parts differ from the *one?* This whole of parts *has*, participates in, the unity that the *one is* — and whatever unity is had by this totality is a derivative of the *one*.[30] Of themselves all the parts are a sheer many — indeed, not even this, for a true many is a multitude of units whereas this is a pure infinite.[31]

This is also true of the single part. It *has* a derivative unity, but we cannot say that it *is* one.[32] Of itself and by itself it suffers the same fate as the whole:

> If we should mentally subtract from the parts even the smallest amount, does it not follow that what is sub-

29. I, 81-82 *et passim*. For an analysis of the logic of Plato which insists it cannot be understood in the light of the concept of substantiality receiving or containing predicates, see Halévy, *La Théorie platonicienne des sciences*, pp. 165 ff. Cf. also Cherniss, I, 316-18.

30. 158a and 158d 3-4.

31. 158b 5 ff.

32. 158a.

tracted is a multitude rather than a one, if it does not share in oneness?[33]

But these parts, into which a part may itself definitively and finitely be broken down, have their derivation and their definiteness from the *One*. Indeed, if this process of division is not in actuality endless, if, for example (at the end of the process of diæresis), we come to an indivisible, an ἄτομον,[34] that cannot be dichotomized, this giving of a pause and a term to the infinite has the same source. But so too with all the inner regions of the division of any concept. At any stage of diæresis we have the possibility of the infinite division of a genus into its subordinate species, thus:

And so with any of the members of this infinite:

S

s s s s s s s s s s s s s s s s s s s s

But the vertical line that is accumulating the elements of the final definition is exceedingly definite and is giving pause to the infinite at every stage of the process. This is due to the constant limiting function of the *one* and *cannot possibly be explained by the power for choice or determination held by each superior genus in the species.*[35] For this power is of itself

33. 158c 2-4.
34. *Sophist* 229d 5. Cf. also *Metaphysics* 994b 21-22.
35. Aristotle himself points out (*Metaphysics* 1037b 19 ff.) that the genus does not properly communicate in its species, for it would then be

infinite and unlimited, and therefore no power at all. We are, therefore, in the presence of one of the principle doctrines of the *Philebus* (the limit and unlimited) and Wundt is perfectly right in associating this hypothesis with the language and the technical achievement of that dialogue.[36]

Our Present Position

How far have we progressed beyond the position of Hypothesis II? In that section we had seen that the original *one* or individual of any kind has moved far beyond its character of absolute indivisibility and, through the characters resident in it of whole and parts, limit and unlimited, has been able to be characterized by all sorts of definite qualities as well as by their contraries. We saw that the presence of contrary qualities within this *one* constituted no serious problem and was not a "metaphysical joke" but rather, in the language of Robin,[37] a development made possible by a more subtle understanding of the principle of contradiction.

Now, as a result of the analysis in Hypothesis III, we see that all the consequences of definite predication and contrariety which belong to the dominant one in any whole belong also to any of its parts.[38] Only we are to remember that both

---

participating in contraries. It cannot, therefore, be the action of the genus that properly decides the particular species, but the action of some whole unit. Here finally Aristotle and Plato seem at one. Does this create a contradiction in the language of the first?

36. *Platons Parmenides*, p. 44.

37. *Platon*, p. 139. It is not necessary to agree with Robin's application of the new subtlety.

38. Cornford admits that the *Others* of this hypothesis may be the parts of any kind of whole, but his major emphasis is on the Others as "Other

their definiteness and their contrariety, as well as their articulation, are completely derivative. At the end of the analysis there remains but one thing which, in the real sense, is of itself definite and predicable. Thus we are well advanced in our study of any one being. The sheer multiplicity we originally saw in this being is only a δόξα, a seeming,[39] which is to be overcome only by the dialectician or philosopher who perceives the all-embracing *one* as alone determining all the predicates contained within it.

There is about this explanation of the structure of essence, I think, as much metaphysical nicety as can be expected of the human mind. For the first time it makes *some* contact with the Neoplatonic explanation that, in this hypothesis, conceives that we are engaged with the entrance of the indivisible *One* into the reality of sense multiplicity. The *one* remains above all division and contrariety while producing all these effects in the many. The explanation of this one-many object also matches in subtlety that of Hegel, whose logic certainly takes the *Parmenides* as one of its most illuminating stimuli.[40]

Ones" in the sensible universe. To my mind, this is the only type of parts in a whole that is probably not referred to. Such parts can exist hypothetically if the rest of the material universe vanishes. But the logic of the hypothesis seems to make this impossible.

39. The word *doxa* here somewhat anticipates Hypothesis VII.

40. Typical examples of the Hegelian interpretation of the *Parmenides* are those of Benjamin Jowett (*The Dialogues of Plato*, IV, 3-42) and Wahl (*Étude sur le Parménide de Platon*). The latter's work falls into this category much more than into the Neoplatonic classification to which Cornford assigns it. It is an extremely competent work and it has thrown light on a number of the hypotheses. The Hegelian reading of the dialogue should not be minimized, and I again feel in general that the logic of Hegel can be of considerable assistance in illuminating this difficult dialogue. The following passage may be cited for its bearing on Hypothesis III: ". . . we mentioned and recalled the dialectic of Plato in the *Parmenides* in deriving

the Many from the One, namely, from the proposition 'One is.' The inner dialectic of the concept has been indicated; and the dialectic of the proposition 'that Many are One,' is most easily taken as external reflection. External it here may be allowed to be, since its object too, the Many, are those entities which are external to one another. This comparison of the Many, each with the other, shows immediately that One is determined just like Other: each is One, is One of the Many, and is by excluding the others; they are simply the same; there is only one determination present. This is the fact, and just this simple fact must now be grasped. Understanding is stubborn in its refusal to accept it only because there is present to it also (and rightly) the distinction; yet the fact mentioned does not eliminate the distinction, and equally the fact exists in spite of the distinction." (Hegel's *Science of Logic*, translated by W. H. Johnson and L. G. Struthers, I [London: 1929], 186.)

8

HYPOTHESIS IV

(159b-160b)

The Problems:

The subject is the indeterminate, or unlimited. A provisional proposal as to the different concepts of the determinate held by Plato and Aristotle.

Of itself, the indeterminate is not one; neither is it a true many (i.e., a numerable set of units). Contrariety involves specific and numerable qualities; hence the indeterminate cannot be like or unlike anything. So with every other contrariety. In every entity, therefore, there is only one principle of unity, from which even the multiple aspects must proceed.

We have now concluded our study of the positive elements of being. In the next four hypotheses we turn to a study of the forms, positive and negative, of non-being in any one.

8

The subject and problem of this section (Hypothesis IV) is the nature of the infinite or unlimited or indeterminate element in any *one*. This is far from being an entirely new theme; the note has already been struck in the second hypothesis, and the infinite divisibility of this element has also been described at length in the third, where its whole capacity for predication and definiteness is seen to come from its association with the principle of oneness. But now we have an entire hypothesis given over in a formal way to an analysis of the indeterminate.

A few preliminary notes are necessary if we are to understand the accurate character and the full range of this principle. A satisfactory sketch of the history of such concepts as chaos, the infinite, the indeterminate, as they occur in Greek poetry, mythology, and early philosophy, has been given by Rivaud[1] and there is no need of retracing this material. Suffice it to say that it seems to be an ineluctable tendency of the mind to conceive that law or God or man are always imposing form and order upon an original confusion. The sophisticated metaphysician accepts the notion for his own purposes, giving

1. *Le Problème du devenir*, Books I and II.

precision to it and resolving the philosophical difficulties that the primitive historical theory creates.

1. As used by Plato, the element of the infinite is universally present in all the fields of the real and is not to be restricted to the world of matter and becoming — as the Neoplatonists restrict it.[2] We have already noted the difficulty of locating it in the world of being, or the Ideas, but have suggested that the infinite logical analysis to which any concept is subject is at least some reflexion, in the logical order, of the possibility of this application. It is only by the constant determining and limiting function of a *one* that infinite divisibility is prevented in the order of actuality. Thus, Stenzel observes that "every logical diæresis, if continued long enough, brings us to an 'indivisible' (ἀδιαίρετον, ἄτμητον, ἄτομον). Otherwise reality would be parcelled up indefinitely, and hopeless skepticism will be the result."[3] I translate "otherwise" here as meaning that which eventuates where the infinite element is conceived of by itself, apart from unity, and this is exactly the supposition of our present hypothesis.

2. Secondly, it has already been noted, but will stand repeating in this more formal discussion of the indeterminate, that such a principle is *essentially* the same in all orders; that is to say, there is an element that fulfills the function of indeterminacy in all being. And the logical system about to be constructed for it in this fourth hypothesis will serve to describe every manifestation of it, whether it be the unlimited

2. For example, Andreas Speiser, *Ein Parmenideskommentar* (Leipzig: 1937), pp. 48-51.

3. *Plato's Method of Dialectic* (translated by D. J. Allan), p. 89.

in the mixture that is Becoming in the *Philebus* or the Receptacle of the *Timaeus* or the completely generalized form of the unlimited that occurs earlier in the *Philebus*. But the infinite of each order differs existentially and numerically from that of any other order. And in this we again correct Aristotle.[4] This holds true both for the limit and unlimited; and this is enough to solve the puzzlement of Demos when he proposes the difficulty that "if we construe the forms as the various modalities of the limit . . . it would follow that the forms are the ingredients of the mixed class . . . this doctrine of the immanence of the forms is hard to reconcile with the doctrine of the absoluteness of the forms." It is perpetually necessary to remember that neither the limit nor the unlimited of the Ideas is identical with the limit or unlimited of sensibles. This proposition saves the transcendence of the Platonic Idea and every element in it. At the same time we are now in a position, after the argumentation of Hypothesis III, to apply the logic of that section not only, as therein, to the relationship between the manyness and oneness of any single entity, but also to the relationship between sensible and Idea. I am referring to the doctrine of participation. In the strictest sense, only the Idea *is;* the sensibles *have* being by participation in the being of the Idea. And this is true of all the elements that compose a sensible. Thus they are entirely different from and entirely the same as the Idea.

4. Georges Rodier (*Études de philosophie grecque* [Paris: 1926], pp. 87 ff.) gives us one attempt to characterize and identify the limit and unlimited as they appear in different orders of being. And I agree with the following remark: "Mais il ne semble pas que la façon dont il introduit la multiplicité dans les Idées contredise sur des points essentiels sa doctrine telle qu'elle est exposée dans les autres dialogues" (p. 93).

Thus, then, we answer the difficulty in the first part of the dialogue, that the multiplication of an Idea in its particulars separates it from itself. If we use the doctrine of participation, we can retort that this is both true and not true. For the meaning of participation may be put thus: it involves a relation between *participant and participated-in* that preserves a difference between them but does not in the strict sense multiply realities; the "and" in the phrase "being and becoming" must be severely qualified.

If we argue in the same direction, the dilemma offered by the "third man" objection against the Ideas will be resolved just as easily and by the instrumentality of the same Platonic theory of participation. "Participated-in" and "participant" cannot be so conceived to be in the one class of entities that it is either possible or necessary to construct a third and finally an endless number of class concepts covering the realities of the Idea and its instances. Strictly, there can never be two such entities as Idea and particular that are unifiable under some common "third." For again the Idea alone *is;* the instances of it have or possess their being by some kind of association with this *one*. There is, therefore, no other Platonic doctrine that so perfectly reconciles the Parmenidean certainty (that the One alone is) with the experiential existence of many sensible particulars.

All these remarks have been evoked by the question whether the indeterminate of numbers, sensibles, and Ideas is one and the same or different.

Hypothesis IV

The Indeterminate and Matter

When we come to the precise nature of the Platonic indeterminate, and to its relation with elements resembling it in other philosophical systems, we are indeed on controversial ground; nevertheless, and partly for the sake of renewing courteous discussion,[5] I will presume to take a very definite stand on a very important point:

By far the most crucial question about the nature and function of the Platonic indeterminate is its relation to the Aristotelian concept of matter. If we were able to settle this problem satisfactorily, we would have a far clearer penetration into the major differences between the ontology and logic of the two systems. We are far from having said the last word here; nor would I even pretend to offer a final solution. Nevertheless, the modern commentator is at least in a position to state some of the things that are fairly clear: one of these is that certainly the ἄπειρον, or unlimited, of Plato is not the ὕλη, or matter, of Aristotle. It is essential to note this—otherwise such an initial misreading of the Platonic notion would ramify into the whole theory of Ideas and produce one distortion after another.

Rivaud goes so far as to say[6] that for anyone who thinks to discover a doctrine of "matter" in the dialogues Platonism

5. Actually, none of the little Plato versus Aristotle debates into which this book has been permitted to enter has any effect on its fundamental interpretation of the meaning of the *Parmenides*. The writer understands that he enters on unsettled territory and he does so in a provisional spirit, quite willing to be strongly countered.

6. See *supra*, chap. 5, n. 16.

must become incomprehensible. Halévy, it seems to me, is equally strong to the same effect.[7] He not only says that it is a mistake to conceive the Idea itself as a subject in which predicates inhere after the manner of a logical subject; he also protests against multiplicity being taken as a *subject* in which unity inheres, and vice versa. Cherniss' recent work is also marked by frequent criticism of Aristotle's identification of the Platonic unlimited with his own "matter," and by an insistence that the two logical and ontological systems are not in any substantial way the same.[8] With all of these I would agree on the radical difference in outlook and method between Plato and Aristotle, and on the two different functions that the infinite or unlimited serves in their writings. The last way in which we ought to interpret any of the forms of the ἄπειρον in Plato — for example, that of the receptacle or χώρα or "space" in the *Timaeus* — is as a previously existing subject "out of which things are composed."[9]

Cherniss tells us that "the orientation of his [Aristotle's] critique of the material principles is toward their character as causes of generation and change."[10] This, I think, is a fair enough summary of the peripatetic notion of matter; it is essentially a substrate, a subject, or something remaining permanently the same but capable of new determination. To this the logic of Aristotle perfectly conforms, with its central notion of a subject receiving predication. Thus, too, with the whole theory of potency and act: each specification of a thing

7. Halévy, *La Théorie platonicienne des sciences*, chap. V *passim.*

8. Cherniss, I, 40-48, 81-82, 171-73, and App. VI.

9. And so agree Cornford, *Plato's Cosmology* (London: 1937), p. 181; Rivaud (see *supra*, chap. 5, n. 16); and Cherniss, I, 171.

10. *Aristotle's Criticism of Presocratic Philosophy*, p. 28.

seems to take the form of a genus-subject in potency to receive a further specifying act. There is, therefore, a constant hierarchical arrangement between elements of the Aristotelian system, a relation of principle and dependent, of ὕστερον and πρότερον.

This is not the method and the emphasis of Platonic thought. The first concern of Plato was not with the metaphysical possibility of change in sensibles. I should say that, so far as particulars go, his concern was with their reality and their unity, with their unity under any and all circumstances, whether viewed statically or dynamically, whether at rest or in motion. We have seen already that, even where he is preoccupied with the study of motion, it is to show that the Parmenidean principle of the One still prevails in an important sense, despite every change. And it is always the doctrine of participation that so dictates the nature of the reality belonging to sensibles that a unity of being is preserved — whether participation is describing the relation of particulars to Idea, or the relation of the members of a sensible unity to the immanent principle of that unity.

We are so accustomed to thinking in Aristotelian terms that we are always conceiving of subjects ready to receive or to generate qualities in the real — and predicates in the logical — order. But this is only one highly special form of relation; it is not pure "relation" itself. As a mathematician would look at it — and Plato was primarily a mathematician and not a biologist — a relation as such between correlatives involves an equality of importance between the correlatives, and this would hold for all the elements that are involved in the unity of any entity in any order (for a unity can be looked upon as a system of relations). A triangle, with its whole complex of lines and angles, gives us a set of elements, all of which are of equal importance in the constitution of its system. No element is a matter in potency toward the actuality of another. The same thing can be said for all the elements of an equation. Thus, too, as we have noticed in Hypothesis III, if a *one* is considered as communicating to the unlimited or unspecified many all their final specificity, the best way of conceiving this internal "operation" within an entity is that the specifying unity descends upon all its elements with equal immediacy, never in such a way that one is a principle or matter or subject of another. It is true that each element in a number series, or in a sensible or definition or Idea, holds a given position in the series of elements, a relation of before and after, but even this position is part of the absolutely unique quality of that element and is, so to speak, part of its self-constitution. It is not determined by the before and after, but by itself—though as a result of association with the *one*.

All these things may also be said of the relation between the Limit and the Unlimited. The latter is not a substratum or subject that is ontologically or logically prior to the former.

The Text of Hypothesis IV

There is no special problem of any kind in summing up the text of this hypothesis. There are no difficult dialectical passages to divide the commentators. For example, Cornford's account is correct; he gets into trouble only in a last unfortunate moment when he misreads the general intention of the whole section. The text gives a description of the unlimited as something that *of itself* can possess no determination, can be specified by neither of two contraries. Plato means to be uncomplicated and he is saying all he says of the indefinite so that it holds whether or not it be in association with a *one*. Even though we have the whole specified and multiplied world of the senses, it would still be true that the "others," as an unlimited, would *of themselves* be unspecified. But Cornford is so intent on his major thesis — that the *Parmenides* is (1) a criticism of the *Phaedo's* emphasis on the separateness of the Forms, (2) an attack on Parmenides, (3) a slow step-by-step generation of the "Pythagorean universe" — that he must finally introduce the following comment:

> We may also see [here] a criticism of Socrates' over-insistence in the *Phaedo* and the early part of our dialogue on the separateness of the Forms. If we take his [Plato's] phrase, 'Unity just by itself' as meaning that the Form Unity is just 'one' and nothing else and is isolated from all combinations with other Forms, it will be in the same class as Parmenides' One. Also the other Forms could not be a plurality of ones; for no other Form could possess unity. Again if Forms are cut off from everything else, they will be cut off from that other factor which might, by acquiring their character, become an individual thing. There will be no "Others" in the sense of concrete and individual things. These can exist only when the unity of the Form acts as the limiting factor.[11]

11. Cornford, *Parmenides*, p. 217.

As a matter of fact, it would be far truer to say the very opposite of all this; namely, that if the *one* were not in nature different from the unlimited, if one were not separated from the other in the sense of being different, then (1) the unlimited would also be one, (2) everything in an entity would be an unqualified unit, (3) we would be back in a world of entities with a completely discrete structure of separate units that have no unity among them, and (4) the whole sense world, with its varieties of one-manys occurring in the phenomena of space and time, would be impossible.

There is, in fact, only one statement being repeated again and again through the fourth hypothesis: only the *one*, or principle of unity in a thing, is one; the others, or members of that unity, are of themselves in no sense one (though oneness may be communicated to them). And this holds true even in the fully structured and determined entity where there is no "separation" and the process of communication and participation may be called complete. Even in that moment the unlimited others still contribute no determination.

We can deny all the contraries in such a "reality" as this Platonic indeterminate — first of all, the fundamental contrariety of a one-many. For if the "others," or the principle of multiplicity, are not one, neither are they a "many," which is nothing save a numerable set of *units*. Further, since there is no quality of determined unity in them they cannot be like, for that would be to possess *one* quality; nor like and unlike, for that would be to have two *unit* qualities. And for the same reason we may say the same thing of all the contrary pairs, whether same-different, or motion-rest, or coming and ceasing to be. They will never be found in the indeterminate.

We could hardly be told more clearly that in any reality or in any order there is only one *one*, and this alone specifies a thing to be what it is, both in its unity and in its multiple aspects. It is this proposition that may be considered the combined achievement of Hypotheses III and IV. And it is not again necessary to indicate at any length how the achievement flows from, and corresponds so much with, the Parmenidean logic. We may finally note that, after the dissection of a *one* that occurs in Hypothesis II, we have in an important sense restored the original unity of an entity as we saw it in the opening hypothesis. *Thus, in the first half of the hypotheses of the dialogue there is a sort of cyclical movement that is now completed.*

It is also helpful to conceive that the eight hypotheses have the following major structural plan: (1) the first four are a positive study of *being*, of the positive elements that enter into any entity, and of the relations between them. This study is now completed. (2) The second four hypotheses constitute an analysis of all the possible forms of *non-being* in a *one*. These forms may be summarized in the following way:

Hypothesis V: Relative non-being, or the Platonic Idea of otherness in a *one*. A being is itself, but *is not* everything else.

Hypothesis VI: Absolute non-being or the complete non-existence of any *one*.

Hypothesis VII: The non-existence that may be described under the Platonic term δόξα; the non-philosophical concept of a *one*. If we conceive that there *is not* a principle of absolute unity in an entity, but only multiplicity, the result is the various confusions of apparent specificity and non-specificity, of being and non-being, that will be described in that hypothesis.

Hypothesis VIII: The absolute non-existence of both the *one* and the many in an entity. This hypothesis is climactic. If there is no *one*, or principle of unity, actually there are no others or many either. So profound is the relation of a *one* to its "others," and so complete the communication of its being to them, that if it does not exist neither do they.

9

HYPOTHESIS V

The Problems:

The subject is relative non-being. The Parmenidean solution of the nature of non-being. The Atomist solution. The Sophistic solution.

When we say in Hypothesis V that the *one* is not, we are talking of the positive one that exists. Here non-being is Otherness, negatively relating a thing to everything else that it is not. This principle of difference or non-being is intrinsic to a being. What is achieved by Plato is the insertion of non-being into the heart of being. This non-being makes multiplicity possible.

The second half of this hypothesis deals with the problem of motion and change. Motion is not Other, but a carefully defined participation in Same and Other.

9

With this hypothesis we begin the Platonic study of non-being in all its forms.[1] For the continuous thread of our discussion through the hypotheses, it is still best to suppose that we are analyzing the laws relative to the nature of a *one*, to the nature of any one thing, in whatever order it is to be found. We must now discuss a whole series of problems that develop from the fact that in some way, indeed in various ways, non-existence is to be found in any *one*. Plato proceeds in these pages to the bold conclusion that every factor thinkable by the human mind is a mixture of being and non-being, same and other, absolute and relative. In brief, Hypothesis V is an anticipation of some of the principal conclusions of the *Sophist* on the relation of being to non-being. It unfolds that dialogue's doctrine of the Other. It is also more than possible, as we shall see, that it goes much further than the *Sophist* by applying its findings to the phenomenon of motion. Finally, unlike Cornford (who has very strong, contrary views on this

1. It is good to repeat here that we were not dealing with a form of non-being in Hypothesis I. That section gave us a description of a *one* precisely as one and nothing else. As one — which everything is — it was unique, indivisible, above all division, involving no relationship, internal or external, not even that of self-identity. It could serve as a description of any unit, from a sense object to the Neoplatonic One. The whole description is positive and valid, but, merely as such, a *one* cannot exist or be known.

hypothesis), I would hold that it is this hypothesis, rather than the third, that gives us the metaphysical basis for the existence of plurality, i.e., for the existence of many *ones*. As a matter of fact, this is the only section of the hypotheses in which the term "Others" may have reference to realities outside the entity represented by the definition of a *one* as studied in all the other hypotheses. But this will not be to say that the second half of the dialogue has at all veered away from its analysis of the nature of *a* one. To be more accurate, it will now unfold an aspect of it that reveals the metaphysical possibility of the co-existence of other realities outside of itself.

Background

The problem of non-being is one of the principal ἀπορίαι, or dilemmas, in Greek philosophy. Perhaps it is the most crucial of them all. There are three special phenomena that caused the question to arise periodically, though the three may somewhat overlap. They are the problems of the negative judgment, of plurality, and of motion or change in general. In negative judgments we are continually saying that that which is is not. Has this non-being any reality and, if so, what is its nature? As for the matter of plurality, if there are many things, then any one thing at the same time simply is, but also is not, i.e., is not things other than itself. As for the phenomenon of motion, some difficulties proceeding from it have already been noted.[2] Can anything be subject to becoming or motion? Can anything that was not come now into being?

2. See *supra*, pp. 51-53. Aristotle summarizes the problem in *Physics* 191a 25 ff.

Not from being, for being already is and cannot become. Not from non-being, for out of nothing nothing comes.[3] But being and non-being seem to be contradictories and to exhaust the whole range of the possible sources of becoming.

Apparently the Greek philosopher, in the face of non-being, was confronted with three possible answers. He might say, as Parmenides did, that non-being simply is not. It can have no relation whatsoever to being and does not exist either inside or outside of being. It is, therefore, in the most absolute opposition to the existent and is its contradictory.[4] We cannot speak or think of it.[5] Here we have a statement of the position that precipitated a full crisis in Greek philosophy—a position that could only be resolved by mediating this complete dichotomy through the combined efforts of Plato and Aristotle.

If we shall omit any discussion of the meaning of the final part of the Poem of Parmenides (the Way of Opinion), the previous section gives us the full revelation of his doctrine on non-being and being. Since the latter completely excludes the former from being present *in* it, being is without parts and indivisible. If there were parts, we would be forced to conceive some part of it as *not being* in another part. Thus it must be the same throughout, a whole and continuous same, without intervals, without beginning or end in time. Therefore interior motion is impossible. But neither can the whole of this

3. The phrase of Melissus (Frag. 1) is: *Οὐδαμὰ ἂν γένοιτο οὐδὲν ἐκ μηδενός* (Diels, *Die Fragmente der Vorsokratiker*, I, 218).

4. *Parmenides* Frag. 8, 15-16; *ἡ δὲ κρίσις περὶ τούτων ἐν τῷδ' ἔστιν · ἔστιν ἢ οὐκ ἔστιν* (Diels, *op. cit.*, I, 236).

5. *Parmenides* Frag. 2, 7-8; *οὔτε γὰρ ἂν γνοίης τό γε μὴ ἐὸν (οὐ γὰρ ἀνυστόν) οὔτε φράσαις* (Diels, *op. cit.*, I, 231).

One Being move, because there is not a non-being outside of it in which it can move.[6] This is the consequence if non-being simply is not.

A second answer — that of the Atomists, for example — would be that there is indeed a non-being but it is completely *outside* of being. The atoms, each one of which is the same full positivity of being that Parmenides assigned to the whole of being, cannot change inwardly. But the real non-being of the void (*κενόν*) outside of them makes motion possible through new combinations of position and arrangement among the atoms. This purely extrinsic non-being has helped to produce change but, faithful to the logic of Parmenides, the Atomist could still answer that being only *is* and has not become. It is unnecessary to indicate here, following the example of others,[7] that this represents an attempt very like in its essential qualities to that of the *Sophist* and the passages of the *Parmenides* we are about to analyze — an attempt to prove the reality of non-being. Nevertheless, it seems in the end to annihilate all true becoming and in its light, as Hegel himself remarks, "all determination, multiplicity, or connection remains a wholly external relation."[8] Nor must we suppose that the problem

6. Melissus presumed to correct his master Parmenides by saying that there is no limit to being and added the note of the infinite. He thought that if there were a limit there would be non-being external to it. Perhaps he was the first to take the sphere simile of Parmenides literally. Despite his praise, Aristotle himself seems to have viewed Parmenides as a *materialistic* monist. See Cherniss, *Aristotle's Criticism of Presocratic Philosophy*, pp. 383-84.

7. Cf., for example, Robin, *La Pensée hellénique des origines à l'Épicure* (Paris: 1942), pp. 70-71.

8. *Science of Logic*, p. 179. For Aristotle's criticism of Empedocles, Anaxagoras, and the Atomists on the same point, see Ross, *Aristotle's Physics* (Oxford: 1936), on 243b 9-10.

had become a purely archaic or historic one by the time of Plato. The Megarians still preserved the traditional monism of the Eleatics, and the "Friends of the Forms" of the *Sophist*,[9] though they are distinguished there from the men of Elea, have introduced the whole of the Parmenidean logic into the separate and diverse Ideas. What we have on our hands, of course, is the great quarrel between the logic of Parmenides and the data of becoming, between the discovery of the One and Being by the mind and of becoming and non-being by sense. The crisis was real enough to generate the skepticism of those Sophists who had begun to teach the third possible answer to the relation between being and non-being; the two are hopelessly the same and all contradictories are equally true.[10] Our complete dichotomy has led to complete identity.

Can the ἀπορίαι of multiplicity, the negative judgment and change, be solved in any other way than these three? The first, very formal attempt at a new solution is growing here in the *Parmenides*. For Plato is the first to insert non-being into the heart of being without identifying the two. True enough, the pages of a dialogue like the *Republic* are replete with the description of a midway entity that is a combination of being and non-being, but these texts[11] deal exclusively with the structure of the world of becoming. The merit of the *Parmenides* is that, as it has promised,[12] it transfers this interior

9. 248a.

10. On Protagoras' denial of the principle of contradiction, see Kathleen Freeman, *The Pre-Socratic Philosophers* (Oxford: 1945), pp. 349-50. Cf. Aristotle, *Metaphysics* 1062b 12 ff. (on Protagoras) and 1062a 31, 1063a 24 (on Heraclitus).

11. For example, 524a, c, 477.

12. 135e ff.

relation to an order of concepts that will hold for all things. Thus far in the dialogue we have dealt with such contraries as One and Many, Like and Unlike, Equal and Unequal, and have seen that, as the specific problem varies, neither or both of these contraries within any one set can be applied to a *one*. It is the business of Hypothesis V to examine the profoundest of all the pairs of opposites and to indicate that both being and non-being can be predicated of any one thing. It will later transfer its findings to the phenomenon of motion in a manner best not anticipated here.

The Platonic Idea of Other

The hypothesis is based upon the condition that "the *one* is not." But Plato goes out of his way again and again to insist that the *one* now in question has a very positive character and that it is not *absolute* non-being we begin to analyze. We are talking of the *one* we have laboriously built up to the present point of discussion, about which many things can be said and about which we now begin to say many negative things. One should observe that the language describing it is completely counter to that used to describe absolute non-being in the *Sophist:*[13] here it is τινὸς . . . τούτου . . . τούτῳ . . . τούτων πάντων τῶν τοιούτων.[14]

We may, therefore, say first that a *one* is what it is, containing a principle of self-identity that can now be called "sameness with self." This is the principle of full positivity and certainly resembles, as far as it goes, the *plenum* of the

13. 238c.
14. 160e 3-4.

Eleatics and Atomists. If we go no further we can say of a *one* that *it is*. Were we to remain in this position, we would be caught in the difficulties of these two logics. We would be told simply that a *one* participates in likeness, by which it is like to itself.[15] The *Sophist* would refer to the same principle under the title of the category of the Same.[16] In this case, sameness with self is an absolute principle and accordingly a *one* can enter into no relation outside of itself.

But a one entity also participates in the Idea of Other. Precisely by being only itself, it is other than, different from, everything else that is outside of it. Otherness is a principle negatively relating a thing not only to its contrary but to everything else that it is not.[17] And where, in a particular negative judgment, a specific thing is negated of a *one* (A is not B) then the negated predicate is only a part of the Different that in its totality would include the rest of the real. Thus, each member of the judgment is *a* part of the Different but *participates* in the whole of the Idea of Difference.

Some of this remains for the *Sophist* to say with greater explicitness, but we are already told in Hypothesis V that Otherness is an *intrinsic* principle in a *one* for "when you say that it is different from other things you do not refer to an Otherness that is in these others but to a factor in itself."[18] Indeed this is also true of all those related qualities that help to indicate the quality of difference in any unity. For a *one* is said to be unlike and unequal to everything else according

15. 161b 5.
16. *Sophist*, 254e.
17. *Ibid.*, 256e 6-7.
18. 160d 8-161e 2.

to the possession of a principle of unlikeness[19] and inequality[20] shared by it intrinsically.

Thus we can now say two things of a *one*. First, "there is knowledge of it."[21] And this means that it is identical, so far as expression goes, with its definition, with all the elements it contains, as an absolute fact of full positivity. But secondly, and this is said in immediate succession, "difference also belongs to it in addition to knowledge."[22] Here we begin to study the definition as a principle of negation and limit and non-being. A *one* is no longer looked at only as a limit but also as a limited. This negative principle is a relational and not an absolute principle — which is always πρὸς τὰ ἄλλα.[23] It exists only by inherence in being. Its foundation is the existence of any two different things. Or, better still, the very foundation of any Other thing is the interior structure of a *one*, that mixture of being and non-being that prevents it from exhausting the whole range of oneness and thus makes multiplicity possible. It is, therefore, purely a relation between *ones* and is a sort of interval separating them. As such it takes the place of the κενόν, or void, of the Atomists.[24] And it is quite

19. 161b 4-6.
20. 161c 9.
21. 160d 5.
22. 160d 8.
23. For example, 161a 6. Cf. *Sophist* 255c 13.
24. For a study of the interval as it is found in the respective doctrines of the Atomists and Plato, see J. Souilhé, *La Notion platonicienne de l'intermédiaire* (Paris: 1919), pp. 37-43, 224-27. There are other interesting questions that can be asked: What is the relation of the *interval* of the *Philebus* (24d) and the χώρα of the *Timaeus*? (Cf. Rivaud, *Le Problème du devenir*, p. 311). And what is the relationship of this χώρα to the void, or non-being, of the Atomists (*ibid.*, pp. 309-10)? Can the ἄπειρον of the *Philebus* (24a–26d) be identified with the ὑποδοχή, or Receptacle, of the

clear that, instead of the external mechanical relation between being and the void, we have on our hands a far more subtle attempt to introduce non-being into the very fibre of being and thus to mediate our original severe dichotomy.[25]

Actually, what we have just seen is the first serious attempt to describe a non-being that is relational (we remember Aristotle's use of the words *logical* and *accidental*). It would perhaps be too much to begin to attach the final system of principles of Aristotle to these findings, but the fact remains that we are here faced with a milestone in the history of Greek philosophy. It is not too much to say that the formation of this concept of relational non-being created a new ontology and logic within which the mind of Aristotle could operate.

The Second Half of Hypothesis V
(*162b 11–163b 7*)

The last section of the fifth hypothesis presents a very special difficulty, as a number of commentators have noted.

Timaeus? (For the literature on the subject, see Cherniss, I, 87.) And the most important question of all is, of course, what is the relation of our Idea of Other to some of these concepts? (See Cherniss, I, 443, who notes that Aristotle "quite unjustifiably" identifies Other with the *Timaeus* Receptacle as well as with absolute non-being.) Finally, as we shall see later, it is certainly wrong to equate Otherness and the Idea of Motion, though Aristotle (*Physics* 201b 16 ff.) does so.

25. I am not suggesting that Plato has the Atomists in mind. It is impossible to reckon the influence of Democritus on Plato, who never mentions him by name. For the literature on possible relations between the two, see Schmid-Stahlin, *Handbuch*, 1, Vol. 2, pp. 331-33. It is possible that the Atomists are being named in *Theaetetus* 156a, *Sophist* 246d, *Laws* 888e.

We can sum it up superficially by saying that it deals with the phenomena of change and motion, and ascribes these, as well as their opposites of rest and changelessness, to the non-existent *one*. It is, of course, difficult to see how in any sense this can be done. Cornford,[26] therefore, is led by the nature of this "appendix" to say that it is impossible for such antinomies to be applied to the positive non-existent Other of the *Sophist* and so would reject our interpretation of the hypothesis. Halévy[27] interprets that the first part of Hypothesis V has resulted in inextricable confusion, for being and non-being have been asserted of the same reality. He therefore proposes that the appendix on motion must be taken as a correction: the contraries of the first part (being and non-being, etc.) can in reality only occur in motion or time; being and non-being can only belong to one same object successively. Wahl, it seems to me, is nearer the truth in accepting the relation to the *Sophist*, but he has not been able to avoid reading into the final section an undiluted Hegelian view.[28]

26. "The confusion of the non-existent entity of this Hypothesis with that 'what-is-not' (τὸ μὴ ὄν) which is identified with 'the Different' in the *Sophist* (257b ff.) was already made by Grote. . . . If we try to interpret the present hypothesis in that sense, the whole of the last section on becoming will be unintelligible" (*Parmenides*, p. 231).

27. *La Théorie platonicienne des sciences*, p. 189.

28. "Mais Parménide n'est pas fini de développer les conséquences de cette hypothèses; l'un étant, puis n'étant pas, n'a pas toujours la même existence; il change, il se meut, dirions-nous volontiers, parce que notre pensée se meut en le pensant, et va du non-être à l'être. Nous retrouvons toujours le même réalisme; puisque nous pensons le non-être, comme étant, ou n'étant pas, il se meut. Le mouvement est projeté de la pensée dans les choses. Ou plus exactement le phénomène — comme pour un James ou en un sense pour un Hégel — est la réalité. Du moment que l'être parait être et n'être pas, c'est qu'il se meut entre ces deux termes." (*Etude sur le Parménide de Platon*, p. 185.)

Hypothesis V

The Question

The principal question is: how shall we reconcile the presence of an appendix on the motion of the non-existent *one* with a view of the latter that equates it with the non-being of Otherness? For this Other is what we might call a purely static relation between diverse entities. And it will not do to solve the matter by asserting, with Aristotle, Xenocrates, and some modern scholars, that Plato identified the Idea of Other with the Idea of Motion.[29] If this identification were valid, there would not be too great a problem in reconciling the two sections of our hypothesis. Actually it is not valid, for Plato explicitly denies in the *Sophist* that the two are one (ἡ κίνησίς ἐστιν ἕτερον τοῦ ἑτέρου).[30]

Nevertheless, I believe that the *Sophist* gives us our best clue for the beginning of a solution to our difficulty. If that dialogue very decisively separates Otherness and Motion, just as decisively does it seem to characterize Motion as the γένος that participates at the same time in both Same and Other.[31] We may gather that this is its unique quality: the participation in such opposing γένη. Motion participates in the Same because, even as all things, it is the same as itself; yet it also participates in Other[32] because it is constantly becoming Other. Every Idea does participate in these two, but Motion, as we

29. For a summary of this point, see Cherniss, I, 442 ff.

30. 256c 5-6.

31. 256a, b.

32. Despite the order in which they are given in the *Sophist*, the γένη of Same and Other are higher in their status than those of Motion and Rest. Hence, Motion can be said to *participate* in them. *Sic* G. Milhaud, *Les Philosophes géomètres de la Grèce* (Paris: 1900), p. 338.

shall see, is a highly special Idea that determines *not only the two elements of motion* (Same and Other) *but also* their mutual relations and the laws of possibility and impossibility *for transition between them.*

Since, according to our view, the special mark of the *one* of Hypothesis V is that it has mediated the dichotomy between being and non-being by fusing the two and by introducing into any *one* a co-participation in Same and Other, there are certainly *prima facie* grounds for supposing that Plato could in this hypothesis associate the two studies I propose he has. There should be no great difficulty in allowing that the phenomenon of motion is, in the order of the dynamic and the successive, the analogue of that which our existent-non-existent *one* is in the order of the "static." Identical co-principles of Same-Other are operating behind both.

A Possibility

One further possibility remains in this whole matter. Our first suggestion has been that structurally motion is the analogue of the non-existent *one*. Therefore, we might suppose that similar metaphysical principles may be established for both, and we should not be shocked if Plato discusses the two within the same hypothesis. The next question to be asked is this: is there any sense in which Plato may have so identified our non-existent *one* with the Idea of Motion that the present appendix involves no change of subject at all? Is it possible that there is a highly generic definition of motion that is constituted by any mutual set of interacting relations in an entity between its sameness and otherness, its being and non-being?

This is not the same as to say that motion, thus understood, would be the general κοινωνία of the γένη and Ideas that some represent as a "dialectical movement." It would rather be restricted to any interplay, static or successive, of Same and Other in any one entity. Actually, we have already seen one Platonic passage that raises some kind of probability for all this. It occurs in Hypothesis II, where it has become clear that a *one* is equated not only with a principle of indivisible wholeness but with the totality of its member parts as well (two things that are identical and different). As one entity is present in one of these principles, it is in itself and in the same as itself; as not contained in the parts, it is in other and in other than itself. But this presence of the One in Other Plato in the earlier text calls motion.[33] This interpretation was there projected as probable.

At any rate, acting on our own hypothesis, we shall set the following course in interpreting the appendix. We shall first apply its dialectic to the non-existent *one* precisely as the latter stands in the first part of the hypothesis. This will then be the generic movement we have just discussed, applied to the static and eternal relationship of logic between Same-Other in any *one*. We shall then apply the logic of the appendix to our own everyday understanding of sensible motion. It is for the second case that the application will certainly hold.

Logic of Motion

The general premise governing the whole section is quickly enunciated: if anything is in a particular state and is not in

33. 145e 4-146a 7.

that state, it is in a state of change[34]—and this is motion. This word "motion" may, therefore, be applied to *any one* that *is* and *is not* ("has not our *one* appeared both as being and not-being?").[35] I am suggesting that here "is not" means "is not something else." Because of this constant shifting between being and non-being, our *one* is in motion. This is the *Sophist's* participation in Same and Other.

But the other part of an antinomy is now expressed. Such a *one* is not in motion and is at rest. The meaning here is difficult but not unfathomable, and the result is a further elucidation of the nature of the relative non-being that is otherness.

Let us suppose that any one thing is a combination of *A* and *not B*. Now if there is to be motion in such a *one*, it is to be found either in *A* or in *not B*.

Consider this *not*, this otherness, as a not-being, resident in *A* and separating it from *B*. The philosopher will consider it as a sort of metaphysical *distance* between essences, which is to be crossed if *A* is to become *B*. But it is a sheer interval that cannot be measured in terms of being, for it is not *A* and it is not *B*. ("It is nowhere among the things that are."[36]) The two places in which it could possibly exist are closed to it by its very nature and, therefore, it cannot be involved in a place-to-place movement. Nor can it move in the one same place for either existential place is closed to it, whether *A* or *B*. ("It nowhere lays hold of the same."[37]) Therefore it cannot move at all.[38]

34. 162b 10-c 2.
35. 162c 3.
36. 162c 7.
37. 162d 2.
38. Note the resemblance of this Other of Hypothesis V to the "instant" of Hypothesis II. The former is the relational being, not measurable in

Plato goes on to say that "the *one* cannot change from itself, whether it is or is not."[39] He has just established that the element of *not B* cannot change. Now he adds that even as existent, as *A*, it cannot be in motion, for *A* is always eternally identified with itself and cannot pass out of itself. Thus, neither of the two elements in *A—not B* can enter into movement.

All this is complication indeed, but all we are asked to remember is the following: (1) In any *one*, there is a sort of motion between its sameness and otherness, its being and non-being. *A* "becomes" *not B*. (2) On the other hand, there is no motion in the reality *A—not B*, nor in the proposition *A is not B*. For we have demonstrated that there is no movement in either of its two terms, either in *A* or in *not B*. If this is a general logic of motion, we should expect that one term of a motion will transform itself into another term, but that at the same time neither will change. There will be a transition from *A* to *B*, but the reality of *A* is never, and never becomes, the reality of *B*. In other words, let us see if, as we apply the appendix to sensible motion, we are now equipped with a logic that will explain "successive" movement.

An Actual Movement

In any actual motion, we have a phenomenon within which a thing becomes its other. Let us sum up any change by saying that "*A* becomes *B*," and let us take as an example the qual-

terms of being, that serves as interval between Ones or essences; τὸ ἐξαίφνης is the interval, not measurable in time, between any two terms of change in time.

39. 162d 5-6.

itative change "White becomes its adjacent color." We must take these total unit phrases as the object of our present study, and in this respect the present passages differ totally from the appendix to the second hypothesis, which we called II A. There our subject was the very point of change and we concluded that of this transitional point neither of the two contrary terms involved in the change can be predicated. The problem here is quite different. We are viewing *the whole process of a change,* and our conclusion will be that both of the two contraries must be predicated of a one in motion or transit. This is still another example of the fact that the *Parmenides* is not meant as an antilogical criticism of all dialectic. It is, once again, a γυμνασία, a training in logic, which is constantly showing that the predication or non-predication of contraries varies with the different problems raised by the nature of any one thing.

Now any process of change does involve some kind of transition from being to non-being, from Same to Other. *A* actually does change to *B*, and this is motion. The whole process is a transition from sameness to otherness. In it we can detect a "being in a certain state" and a "not being in that state."

On the other hand, we seem to be warned that we must qualify this movement and must also indicate all the senses in which there is no motion in the different elements involved in any such process. Let us regard the non-existent *one* as *A* or *White* and its non-existence as *not B* or *not-Black.* Not-Black is the non-measurable interval of otherness between the movement terms of White and Black. It must be crossed if one is to become the other. Now Plato wishes to tell us of this interval that it is absolute and that it is non-measurable. It is absolute because actually the reality of White can never become the reality of Black. A *one* is always itself and cannot change into its other (οὐδὲ μὴν ἀλλοιοῦταί που τὸ ἓν ἑαυτοῦ[40]). Another color may come out of White, but we have already been forbidden in the *Phaedo*[41] to think that one quality is the "material out of which" another is formed. *We cannot build a philosophy of a moving one that would be the death of all logic, that would equate all things with their opposites.*

Therefore, too, it is equally necessary that the otherness between any two beings not be measurable in terms of being. There is no midway region between qualities (or *ones*), where one would slowly become the other. The absolute difference between Ideas, for example, is saved by there being literally a nothing between them. The same thing is said in another way in the *Sophist*,[42] where we are told that all becoming is always according to completeness and according to wholes (τὸ γενόμενον ἀεὶ γέγονεν ὅλον). How Aristotle himself leaned on these teachings to explain alteration, by protecting the principle of excluded middle, should be plain. The logical problem involved in motion is solved for him by the instantaneity of change, the indivisibility of the interval of change, and the immutability of its terms.[43]

40. 162d 5-6.
41. *Phaedo* 103.
42. 245d 4.
43. See *Physics* 224b 25 ff., 235b 32 ff. See also Cherniss, *Aristotle's Criticism of Presocratic Philosophy*, pp. 89-90, and Ross, *Aristotle* (London: 1949), p. 175.

One Last Question

One last question remains to be asked. Are we helped at all toward a general theory of motion in Plato by supposing that motion, in whatever order of things it is found, must always indicate a reference to some fusion of Same-Other?

The three elements in a Platonic theory of motion must be (1) the Idea of Motion, or the model, (2) the self-movement of soul, or the mover, and (3) the final or lowest form of motion, that of phenomena.

Undoubtedly the Idea of Motion itself is not in motion. Nor is it the immediate cause of motion. It is the transcendent pattern of all movement, constituted by a system of elements and by the relations existing between them. These elements are Same and Other; the relations are the antinomic possibility and impossibility of passage between them. Thus, we should not ask how the logic of movement we have been summarizing applies to this Idea, for the two are in one sense the same, the logic being in the order of expression what the Idea of Motion is in the order of the transcendent. Both are the models of all actual motions. If we were to take the Idea as *a* particular motion then it would not stand as a principle outside the group of all particular movements, and we would be confronted by a legitimate argument of the "third man" type.

Soul — as the mediating principle between the Idea of Motion (indeed, between all the Ideas) and physical phenomena — looks to the former as model of the motion the soul induces in the latter. It differs from sensible movement by reason of being self-movement (this is its very essence[44]) and of being cause of all other movements. But it, too, is a being that is essentially composed of Same and Other. Perhaps, therefore, we should put aside a possible preoccupation with epistemological reasons for the presence of Same and Other in the Soul (like is known by like) and consider whether these elements are placed in it so that it be *par excellence* the manifestation of motion and the cause of it in others.[45] Without the soul there is no motion, but without Same and Other there is no soul.

Finally, though the movement in the order of becoming is an inferior movement, communicated, spatial and temporal, it does not follow that our logic of motion does not apply to it as formally and essentially as it does to the soul. The diversity between the two, even with regard to their participation in the general categories, has been carefully elaborated by Plato in the *Timaeus*,[46] and the commentary of Proclus[47] should have protected these differences once and for all. But despite all the differences one thing remains true: wherever a *one* is in motion, in whatever order, it will follow the pattern of the logic and the Idea of Motion we have generally indicated.[48]

44. *Laws* 896a.

45. "This Idea, then [of motion] was not conceived as the 'class' of all physical changes or as the 'abstract type' of any of them but as the absolute reality which manifests itself in the positive self-motions which are souls." (Cherniss, I, 441. Cherniss' discussion of motion and the soul [376 ff.] is exhaustive.)

46. 35a ff.

47. *Commentarius in Platonis Timaeum* (Vratislaviae: 1847), pp. 184 ff.

48. Cornford's position on this hypothesis (which he refuses to associate with the Idea of Other in the *Sophist*) is so strongly taken that I should

like to add a final note on his argument. I very much respect his handling of the evidence but must question it in places. He is intent on proving that the hypothesis deals with a non-existent One about which, however, many true things can be said and which can come into existence, can become. As I see it, the hypothesis *does* deal with otherness, but in such a way as to help us toward a fuller theory of becoming and motion. Cornford makes much of the content of 162b 10 ff., which includes the central words of transition and motion. For him these words involve a new point of discussion, where the non-existent one is conceived of as passing into existence. One trouble with seeing this as a new state for the One is the past tense *ἐφάνη* (162c 3): "we have seen" that the one both is and is not. I do not understand how he has a right to call this phrase "ambiguous" and then "support" his reading of it by the equally difficult phrasing of 162d 6, which he questionably translates as "*when* existent or *when* non-existent." Both places can be referring to any existing one that has in it an element of being and of non-being or otherness. Moreover, in the crucial lines of 162c, where Plato might have been expected to state his "new point" fairly unequivocally, his phrasing is "transition from being to non-being," not the reverse, though the reverse is not excluded. I would also question Cornford's firm reading of 161c. The passage could just as well mean that, until and unless we regard an existent entity as having in it an element of non-being, we cannot establish it as unequal or unlike anything else. If we regarded it as only *being*, we would be back in all the old Parmenidean difficulties. As long as all things simply *are*, they are all alike and one! But may I fall back on a simplicity that is not so much an a priori argument as a matter of common sense? It is difficult to admit that, if Plato is devoting four substantial hypotheses to the problem of the non-being of the One, he should nowhere within them have studied the form of non-being called "otherness," that the doctrine of the *Sophist* should not have been *here* anticipated, but should have appeared only later, full-armed like Athena. It is as difficult to think in this way as it is to reject the authority of Mr. Cornford, especially when he has himself elsewhere pointed out the anticipation of this doctrine (*Parmenides*, p. 159).

10

HYPOTHESIS VI

The Problems:

The subject is absolute non-being. We are talking of a one that in no way is. This hypothesis marks the fifth different denial of the predicability of either of two contraries. In this case the reason is simplest of all, and yet a form of definition of the "thing" under discussion: nothing can be predicted of nothing. This hypothesis marks the second denial of knowability, but unknowability also has different bases. When we say a pure one cannot be known (Hypothesis I) and that nothing cannot be known (Hypothesis VI), we say two different things.

10

Now that Plato has untied one of the Gordian knots of pre-Socratic philosophy by this exposition of the existence and nature of relative non-being, he can afford to be completely free and uninhibited in the description of the absolute non-being of a *one* that follows. The classical distinction between the two forms of nothingness having been made, it is now possible to repeat and to accept — at times in almost literal fashion — everything that Parmenides has said of pure nothingness. And this is exactly the function of Hypothesis VI.

For Plato's complete doctrine of absolute non-being we should have to examine the joint contributions of this and the final hypothesis of the dialogue. For the two stand close to each other in a tightly knit fashion. First of all, in the sixth, if a *one* is not (i.e., if there is simply no principle of unity in an entity), what can be said of this *one?* Nothing. It exists in no way, has no relation to being, cannot be described by either of any two contraries, and cannot be the object of thought. This in sum is the message of the sixth hypothesis. The final hypothesis goes much further: it announces that if there is not such a principle as a *one* then neither does the principle of manyness or the infinite or the "others" exist.

There is literally and absolutely nothing. Let us therefore remember that the present brief discussion limits itself to the *one,* and reserves the full consequences of the positing of its non-existence to the final page of the dialogue.

The distinction between the two types of non-being is clearly drawn at the very beginning of the present analysis. We are not now talking of the type that has been analyzed in Hypothesis V (which "in one sense is not and in another sense is"[1]), but of something that "has no share whatsoever in being."[2]

We are no longer concerned with relative non-being. For this is no more than a principle in a *being* by which it is limited to self-identity and is not anything other than itself. Such a principle also has being. It involves the existence of a *one.* Thus the discussion in Hypothesis V is eminently positive: it asks the question, how shall we limit an entity that really *is?* But now we suppose that this *one* does not exist at all. Then it cannot lose being, for it does not have it to lose (which is Eleaticism in reverse: non-being, or the loss of being, cannot come from non-being); nor can it come to be (for out of nothing nothing comes). Nor can it be altered, for this is but a form of coming and ceasing to be. It cannot move, for that is a form of alteration; it cannot be at rest, for this is a designation for *being* in the Same. Finally, we cannot attribute to it any of the contraries. And here we locate it within the constantly varying law of predication that runs throughout the eight hypotheses. Like the *one,* or principle of complete indivisibility, of Hypothesis I; like the instant,

1. 163c 4-5.
2. 163c 6-7.

or point of change, of Hypothesis II A; like the unlimited, or principle of multiplicity, of Hypothesis IV — this pure nothing can receive neither of two contrary predicates. The law of predication is the same in every case. But the inner soul of this law, its rationale, is completely different from all these other examples. All these other principles are real principles, and the negative predication in each instance is a means of *defining* their type of reality. But here the negations are based on the absolute non-being of the "subject." And it is in this respect that I differ most strongly with the reading of Cornford, who tortuously interprets that the words "one" and "others" are always changing their meaning and are thus producing new types of predication. I hold that we are always talking of precisely the same "one" (of any unity in the world) and precisely the same "others" (the elements of *that* one); it is the law of predicability that is always shifting as we discuss various aspects or elements of a *one* or, as in this case, we speak of it as an unreality.

Plato ends this analysis of sheer non-being by repeating the Parmenidean formula that it is unthinkable, it cannot be the object of thought. He agrees with Parmenides that what can be thought and what is are one and the same; what is not cannot be thought. This is the second time we have denied something the possibility of its being known, the first being at the conclusion of Hypothesis I. This, therefore, is as good an occasion as any other to repeat the totally different grounds in each case for the denial of the possibility of knowledge.

We have just witnessed an analogue of this problem. In the eight hypotheses there are five different denials of the predicability of either of two contraries, and the reason is that different realities or phenomena within a *one* are under discussion. Thus, too, there are altogether different reasons for our two failures of knowledge. In Hypothesis I knowledge fails because the subject is real (the principle of indivisibility in a *one*) but "unknowable" in the technical Platonic sense. It is precisely its indivisibility that causes its unknowability. In the present hypothesis the unknowability is as absolute as the non-being involved. Plato has already referred at least twice to this type of unknowing. In the *Euthydemus*[3] he has said that "no one speaks what is not"; in the *Republic*[4] he again refers to the nature of pure non-being and to the ἄγνοια which is its correlative; finally, the subject is, of course, elaborately discussed in the *Sophist*.[5]

I cite this repetition of the fact of unknowability because to my mind it is at least a small corroboration of our reading of the all-important first hypothesis. It is not Plato's fashion, in these eight hypotheses, to analyze the same problem twice over. The knowledge problem of Hypothesis VI is not the same as that of Hypothesis I. In the latter we are dealing with an indivisible that is quite real but that cannot be known until it becomes the Whole of Hypothesis II. Human knowledge grasps two things in a single glance, the one and its many. And if one should retort with the objection of the *Theatetus* that from this standpoint the *one* is a single "element" or στοιχεῖον, the parts all single elements, and thus all of them, separate or together, are unknowable, the answer

3. 286a.
4. 477a 2-4.
5. 238c ff.

has already been given many times by Plato. The *one* and many in a knowable entity are not different but the same. Halévy puts the case very well by suggesting that the principle of unity is nothing but a relational system of the parts, and these parts are in no sense different from the system.

11

HYPOTHESIS VII

The Problems:

The subject is δόξα, or opinion, the way in which the ordinary man, the non-metaphysical man, regards reality—with the senses alone. The seventh hypothesis follows the mind of the man who does not philosophically acknowledge an indivisible principle in every entity and yet tries to hold onto the definite multiplicity and parts that come only from this principle.

Again we ascribe both of two contrary predicates to our subject, but only by aping the valid logic of previous double predications. The collections or masses of being seen by the doxastic mind only seem to be one; again they only seem to be true multitudes. A logic of real unity would make them such, but not the logic of δόξα.

There is no original chaos, or confused intermixture of the contraries, existing before the *one*.

11

We have said before that one of the most fruitful ways of understanding the *Parmenides* is to see the dialogue as an overhauling and reshaping of the Parmenidean logic. To say, as many do, that it is anti-Eleatic is very much to oversimplify the whole problem. Plato has a basic reverence for the figure of Parmenides and this can only mean a basic respect for him as a metaphysician. Actually, Plato's attitude is constantly shifting between fidelity and correction.

Thus, fidelity is the note in Hypothesis I where, contrary to every manifestation of multiplicity in any *one,* Plato asserts that the fundamental factor in any entity is an absolute indivisible — to which we can ascribe neither parts nor extremes, nor inner differentiation, and about which we can say practically all that Parmenides has said of his One Being. Somewhat the same thing occurs in the third hypothesis. There we saw that in any *one* there is only one true being, and this is the one. The *one* is all-pervading and its member-elements receive from it all their definiteness as factors. To say, in any sense of addition or mixture, that there is a *one and a many* is sheer simplification. Even within an Idea only the *one* in any complex *truly is*, and all the member-Ideas in that complex have being only by participation.

There are, of course, modifications of Eleaticism, and these are of a very serious character. Hypothesis II has developed the very intricate character of any real unity. The concept of the Whole replaces the simple notion of a *one*, and the fundamental contrariety of One and Many, Limit and Unlimited, produces an endless number of derivative contraries in any unity. But in a still more precious way it is the fifth hypothesis, with its doctrine of a real non-being, limiting a *one* and introducing the possibility of other *ones* and of multiplicity, that has broken one of the essential Gordian knots of the Eleatic logic.

In the case of the hypothesis we now begin to discuss, I am going to suggest the helpfulness of regarding it as a modification of still another Parmenidean mode of thought. Specifically I refer to his critique of δόξα, of the way in which the ordinary man, the non-metaphysical man, regards reality. The unphilosophical man never sees anything but some kind of multiplicity, he never penetrates to oneness or the indivisible, never discovers the εἶδος. The *one* is the territory of the philosopher. Therefore, when Plato again proposes in the present hypothesis that *a one is not*, he is actually placing himself introspectively in the soul of the "doxastic" man and is asking himself what is left of reality for such a mind to grasp. And the whole course of the hypothesis is rendered intelligible by understanding that even what he thinks he grasps is in reality not there. In other words, we are to be given another rigorous criticism of the doxastic, the unexamined way of thought, after the tradition of such men as Heraclitus, Parmenides,[1] and Democritus.

Parmenidean Δόξα[2]

Let us suppose that the most general signification of the word δόξα is this: it represents that unphilosophical perception of reality that does not grasp the essence or unity behind the multiplicity and mutability of phenomena. In general, it is the view of the world that remains when unity and fixity have not been discovered in it, or have been abstracted from it. To follow the course of the Eleatic conclusion would be to say that, assuming the failure to posit the Parmenidean One, the world he describes as the Way of Opinion would

1. For the attitude of both Heraclitus and Parmenides toward popular knowledge, see Diels, *Parmenides, Lehrgedicht* (Berlin: 1897), pp. 68 ff. ("Der Eleate wie der Ephesier, beide sind entschiedene Gegner des Sensualismus," p. 69). Diels notes two attacks on the ignorant in *Parmenides:* the first is against the general mass of men, who confuse being and non-being; the second, he judges, is against the Heracliteans, who assert these two to be both the same and not the same. But Cornford ("Parmenides' Two Ways," *Classical Quarterly*, XXVII [1933], 99, n. 3) rejects the whole identification of Frag. 6, 4-9, of Parmenides' poem with Heracliteanism. This second way of seeming is for him simply the general "way of mortal belief based upon sense experience" (p. 100). At any rate, it is at least possible that Plato, in this present hypothesis, has Heraclitus also in mind. Neither he nor Aristotle seems to have paid much attention to the element of unity—whatever its final metaphysical intent—in him. Does Plato, therefore, think of Heracliteanism when he says "if the one is not"?

2. For a summary of δόξα in Parmenides, see Cornford, *op. cit.*, p. 100: "Δόξα or τὰ δοκοῦντα . . . includes (a) what *seems real* or 'appears' to the senses; (b) what *seems true;* what all men, misled by sensible appearances, believe, and the δόγματα philosophers have taught on the same basis (for in the mouth of a goddess 'mortals' includes philosophers); and (c) what has *seemed right* to men . . ."

remain. Actually, this Way is, in briefer form, as much a scientific summary of the then existing experimental knowledge of the world as the *Timaeus* was to be for Plato. At any rate, in it the whole content of the Way of Truth — with its description of Being as One, continuous, undifferentiated, indivisible, the same throughout — is negated and we have the world of specificity, difference, and change that is the truth for the ordinary human eye. Assuming as a probability that this Way of Opinion is rejected by Parmenides, his position would seem to be that which has already been indicated: there is only a Being which is absolutely One; but if this were not so, if you reject this One, you have the completely differentiated world of δόξα on your hands.

Platonic Δόξα

On the other hand, the hypothetical removal of the Platonic One from the picture is far more radical in its consequences than the removal of the Parmenidean One, so far as concerns the doxastic view that remains. We must remember that, while in one sense the Platonic One is obviously less absolute than the Parmenidean, in another sense it is more so. Any Platonic *one* is a multiple and highly differentiated complex, but this multiplicity *and* specificity is completely *derivative*[3] from the principle of oneness in an entity. If, therefore, you place yourself beyond the view of the One, you must be faithful to your

3. It is difficult to express this truth without Neoplatonic implications. But I think that this relationship of complete dependence between the member factors in anything and their principle of unity will be further clarified by the final hypothesis.

premise and follow the hypothesis to the hilt. Wherever you are doxastically holding onto some form of the multiple and the differentiated, actually you still hold onto some dimly philosophical explanation of a *one* that is the source of such differentiation. Consequently, as you are progressively stripped of this explanation, all differentiation within any one entity successively vanishes; finally you are left with a completely undifferentiated reality within which all the members of contrary pairs are confounded with each other. Δόξα, as a matter of fact, never becomes entirely consistent, for if it did it would find that it had completely abandoned philosophical unity and had fallen into the complete impasse either of non-being or, at least, of that kind of complete indeterminate that has already been scientifically sketched for us in Hypothesis IV. But of its very nature it stands on a midway ground, ever holding onto scattered perceptions of unity and differentiation, but always allowing these to be further dissolved.

The consequence of all this is that in Hypothesis VII we must retrace our steps and consider more carefully what Plato means by the original premise that "a *one* is not." The sense in which this is premised makes our study of VII totally different from that of IV and VIII. In Hypothesis IV, there is a complete separation of the One from its members, with the result that the latter reach the stage of the completely indeterminate and have *no* specificity. In Hypothesis VIII, we shall presently see that a total non-existence is supposed for all unity, as a consequence of which not only all differentiation but any kind of reality is denied to the compositional elements of a *one*. Where, then, is there ground for the creation of this seventh hypothesis? For what else can be said of a *one* negatively save that it is either separated from the Others or does not exist at all? (And what else can be said of the Others in consequence save that they either become wholly indeterminate or do not exist at all?) These questions can only be answered when we understand that in the present case oneness is posed as non-existent after the indecisive manner of doxastic thought. And that Plato is now analyzing this kind of thinking is more than hinted at, even by the evidence of purely surface clues. For in no more than sixty-four lines of text, the word "seems" (or "appears" or some other equivalent) occurs no less than twenty-five times.

Essentially some inferior kind of thinking is the manner of all δόξα. According to its most steadfast meaning in the dialogues, it is a faculty midway between knowledge and ignorance and, consistently with the Platonic habit of defining a faculty by its object,[4] the object of *doxa* is the mixture of being and non-being that is the status of becoming.[5] In accordance with the very nature of its object, its conclusions are never fixed;[6] its virtue and goodness are inferior;[7] its courage is without wisdom;[8] its poetic insights are highly

4. *Republic* 477a.

5. It is in this more general sense that I use the word throughout this chapter (see *Republic* 477), not in the most carefully guarded sense in which it is distinguished from αἴσθησις in the *Theaetatus.* But it would be still more accurate to say that I take the word as Plato opposes it to εἶναι and εἰδέναι, in the sense in which it means "to appear" but not really "to be." For instances of this use, cf. Souilhé, *La Notión platonicienne de l'intermédiaire*, pp. 77-78. Thus, in this hypothesis we shall come across the phrase ὄντα οὐκ ἀληθῶς φαίνεται (164e 2-3). But obviously δόξα does not always have a pejorative sense in the dialogues.

6. *Meno* 98a.

7. *Phaedo* 69a, 64d ff.

8. *Laches* 192-193.

limited;[9] its political insights are based on shifting opportunism; and its most accurate physical discoveries can never have the exactitude of true knowledge.[10]

But the δόξα of which there is now question is more widely ranging than any of these concepts. For the *one* that we are analyzing through all the hypotheses is the notion of oneness as such and is representative of unity in any order. But the concepts of δόξα that we have just enumerated restrict themselves to the order of becoming and to the obscurities that essentially reside in it. Now we deal with a δόξα (with all its limitations and imprecisions) that can invade any order of things, whether that of becoming or that of the Ideas. There is a type of imprecision of which even those who believe in the Idea can be guilty. Thus we are told in the *Sophist*[11] that only he who accurately divides the kinds is the true philosopher; but, even more importantly, we are warned in the *Philebus*[12] that we must not go too quickly from the indeterminate to the final, completely differentiated *one*. If we do, the sense is, kind will merge into kind and the result will be considerable obscurity of definition. The *one* will not have been allowed to produce a definite number of factors and we shall be left with an impression of any one entity that is similar to the very general description of the vague impression of "seeming" Plato is about to give us in detail. We turn now to the text, hoping that the above will largely clarify the direction of the successive steps in the seventh hypothesis.

9. *Ion* 536b, d; *Apology* 22a, c.
10. See chap. 3, n. 48; also *supra*, n. 5.
11. 253d, e.
12. 17a.

The Text of Hypothesis VII

If in thought we now separate a *one*, or unity, from the "others," or members of that unity, what kind of reality is left to these others? Let us see how, once granted this separation, we can know the latter.

By "others" we mean members of a *one* that are really specific and distinct, and that are known to be such. They are the whole, inwardly articulated structure of any entity. Difference pervades all of it, but the whole problem is: will this difference survive if oneness is taken away? Let us introspectively follow the course of the mind of the man who does not philosophically acknowledge an indivisible unity in all things:

The articulation or otherness in a thing does not proceed from a difference between the others and the *one* — for by hypothesis there is no such *one*.[13] Well then, the others are simply other than one another.[14] Not that each one is distinguished from another, for they cannot occur as ones or units; again by hypothesis there is no such thing.[15] Let us say, therefore, that they combine together in groups or "masses" and that each such bundle of being differs from any other.[16] Thus we seem to have introduced *some* clarity into the picture of the others — unless this clarity will also vanish under the pressure of fidelity to our premise. And surely enough it begins to vanish! Evidently we have still been holding onto the concept of the definite, and therefore of the one; so that if

13. 164c 4-5.
14. *Ibid.*
15. 164d 7-e 3.
16. 164c 8 ff.

now we drop this hold then the beginning of one aggregate finds a new beginning, but pays the price of merging into still another beginning.[17] And at the interior of such a grouping we must try harder to give up all sense of *definite* and unitary otherness, because every line or point of interior articulation can be broken down into further divisibility,[18] and so on indefinitely. What we must do is continue to dissolve all definiteness and all unity. Nevertheless, we shall never quite come to the moment of complete dissolution at which we shall have reached such an ἄπειρον as is described in Hypothesis IV — for that is to be decisive indeed and can only be the object of the vision of the true philosopher. And that, perhaps, is why Plato says that the "indeterminate" of the *Timaeus* is among the things to be grasped by intelligence, even though a bastard intelligence.[19] Let us in sum describe the present kind of knowing by the phrase which Plato himself uses:

> We shall always find that what we have before us is a mass without a unit.[20]

This notion of a "mass without a unit" is of course confusing and impossible, but it represents the kind of thinking that supposes you can have even the specificity of the world of perception without some kind of doctrine of oneness; that you can have aggregates, even roughly defined, without *ones*.

17. 165a 9-b 2; cf. the interesting discussion of this section by Damascius, in Ἀπορίαι καὶ λύσεις περὶ τῶν πρώτων ἀρχῶν εἰς τὸν Πλάτωνος Παρμενίδην (Paris: 1889), p. 318.

18. 165b 2-3.

19. *Timaeus* 52b 2.

20. 165b.

The Problem of the Contraries in Δόξα

We have seen that with each new problem studied in the eight hypotheses a new version of the predicability or non-predicability of contraries emerges for any *one*. The remaining lines of Hypothesis VII now state the "laws" of contrariety for the mental world of δόξα. But these laws can only be understood insofar as they are seen to be imitations (and confused imitations at that) of the logic of contraries that has been set up in previous hypotheses. It is, therefore, necessary to review certain of these still another time.

In the first hypothesis, all predication is impossible to a *one*, because it is viewed there as an absolute indivisible; if even self-identity involves some kind of duality, then even self-identity is lacking to it. In the second hypothesis, this indivisible now emerges as a whole, first of all as a complex of unity and being, and then of further elements. It is, indeed, composed of a "finitizing" and an infinite element, each carefully distinguished and yet identical with the other — and out of this fundamental contrariety emerges a whole succession of contrary predicates. In the third hypothesis, the net result, so far as concerns our present point, is that this possibility of contrary predication is to be applied validly to each definite part of the whole complex, and for the same reason: that, as a result of union with the *one*, each is a composition of limit and unlimited. The set of contrarieties that then develop are identical with those of Hypothesis II. But so is the list which Plato now gives for δόξα in Hypothesis VII; *except the truth is that they only ape the valid logic of these previous sections.*

Hypothesis VII

By hypothesis just one of the fundamental contraries — the others or the infinite — is present, and only by confusion and by infidelity to the premise is the second — the *one* — there at all. Let us examine the results:

We see a "mass" of being and yet it is not truly such. We *think* we see one thing but in reality it turns into a multiplicity (whereas in the previous hypotheses we were actually in touch with a true *one* and a true multiplicity, the reality of each of which was based on separate factors). So, successively, these false "masses" each appear to be finite and infinite, similar and dissimilar, identical and different. *They will appear to be discrete unities over against each other, but in the next glance of the eye, because of the absence of the one and of the specificity it would by its presence create, they will appear to be running into each other and thus be a sort of confusing continuum of all the elements in any one thing. And so on with all the other contraries.*

Thus, if we had been consistent according to the consistency of the Eleatic logic, either we would have seen any one thing as a thoroughly homogeneous entity (only being or sheer unity would remain); or if we had cancelled such a One, then we would have been faced with nothing but absolute non-being. If, on the other hand, we had chosen the Platonic logic, it would have been dealing with a world of *ones* that are thoroughly unified *and* thoroughly articulated. However, δόξα has attempted to keep this articulation and otherness without unity. The consequence should have been a completely indeterminate being without any definite factors. Actually, the result of its curious compromise is a confusion of the contraries. And for the first time in the dialogue we have come across an illegitimate and impossible predication of contrary pairs.

An Ontological Interpretation

One serious difficulty intervenes against the above interpretation. It can be stated very simply:

There seems actually to be a region of being which for Plato might correspond fairly closely to the relativity and confusion that is the mark of δόξα. The evidence for such a reality is drawn from the *Philebus, Politicus,* and *Timaeus.* These dialogues picture for us a world where contrary is actually opposed to contrary, but in a manner so indistinct and undetermined that the antinomical predication we have just reviewed seems entirely warranted by it. Let us therefore again resume our case from the beginning.

If we take our hypothesis as a purely ontological problem, then Plato is saying that if from any complex whole we remove the factor of oneness we have as remainder a group of "others" that are related to one another as vaguely defined masses. Actually, these bundles of being have no precise boundaries, inner or outer, and their discreteness is constantly transforming itself into a continuum. This shifting between contraries, between discrete and continuous, finite and infinite, one and many, seems to indicate that the contraries run into each other and produce not merely the appearance but also the reality of opposite predicates, though it be in the mixed mode we have indicated. Does this correspond to anything in the ontology of Plato? On the surface it would seem so.

The *Parmenides* itself has already provided us (in Hypothesis IV) with the precise formulation of the notion of a completely indeterminate factor in being. The great myth of the *Timaeus* presents us with a picture of three fields of the real: the world of the Ideas, of γένεσις, and of χώρα. This last is the receptacle of being, this "place in which" (not "out of which") becoming is formed.[21] With it we again meet a complete indeterminate, capable therefore of receiving all forms of the definite; it is, as it were, thoroughly unprejudiced.

This is satisfactory enough and, though there are serious puzzles about the exact meaning of this receptacle, it is at any rate the concept of a philosophical mind. But now something distinctly non-metaphysical intervenes to cloud the picture. This takes the form of an original chaos in the receptacle, in which sensible qualities are already dimly present[22] — "*tending to group themselves vaguely in indefinite masses*, so that you say that one part is 'fiery,' another watery . . . the qualities are grouped in pairs of opposites; if they are to exist at all, one part of the whole mass must be hotter, another colder; one drier, another moister and so on."[23] Cornford compares this Platonic chaos to that of Anaxagoras and cites Fragment 4: "All things being together, not even any color was discernible; that was prevented *by the confusion of all things* — of moist and dry, hot and cold, bright and dark."[24]

This is all antecedent to any influence of the Ideas being

21. For a fuller description of the distinction "in which" and "out of which," see Rivaud, *Le Problème du devenir*, p. 298.

22. *Timaeus* 52d ff.

23. Cornford, *Plato's Cosmology* (London: 1937), p. 202. (Italics are mine.)

24. *Ibid.*

brought to bear upon the receptacle. And if this purely *physical* description of the nature of the indeterminate is being given full credit by Plato, then the *metaphysics* of the *Parmenides* would make no sense at all. Actually though, there is no real problem here, for the very great majority of commentators[25] are agreed that the temporal sequence of events in the *Timaeus* is not to be taken seriously but is an example of the didactic breakdown of a metaphysical structure into an imaginative representation of its elements. It is the imagination that has intervened to substitute the raw material of a *vaguely formed* chaos for the concept of a complete indeterminate that will receive all its specificity from various principles of oneness called "the Ideas." Thus the presence and confusion of qualities and contraries is really the result of the mind already vaguely insinuating unity into its understanding of indefiniteness.[26]

25. For a list of such views, see Cherniss, I, 424, n. 357.

26. A dialogue like the *Timaeus* will lead us astray many times if we do not understand it as a myth that is always *putting things together* that never were or could be separated, that is pedagogically and imaginatively *constructing* things never made, that is, therefore, introducing time into the eternally true or eternally existent. It is a highly conscious use of *δόξα*. In the explanation of indetermination, a first confusion of factors and qualities is the most accurate picture the imagination can form. In this we borrow from the early myths and from the pre-Socratics. For some of the sources of this "essentially poetic notion," see Rivaud, *op. cit.*, pp. 84 ff. Aristotle himself uses the word *μῖγμα* of the *ἄπειρον* of Empedocles and Anaxagoras (e.g., *Physics* 187a 22). But it is the essential business of the *Parmenides,* as we have said (see *supra*, pp. 71 ff.), to be metaphysically precise. Very often Plato is treating the same problem in the *Parmenides* and *Timaeus*—in the one as metaphysician, in the other as myth-maker. Aristotle (*De Caelo* 279b 32-280a 11) took the myth literally, but in this he differs from most of the members of the Academy. For recent but divergent comments on the matter, see J. F. Callahan, *Four Views of Time in Ancient Philosophy* (Cambridge: 1948), pp. 32-37.

Let us now transfer this analysis to the *Philebus* and *Politicus*. There we meet the beginnings of an analogous situation. It seems to me, however, that the doctrine of the indeterminate of these dialogues has special reference to an indeterminate that is the property of each specific Idea. In the *Timaeus*, we talk of a field of indefiniteness into which all qualities and all contraries can enter. Restrict the field to any one quality or pair of contraries and you have a more proper understanding of the unlimited of the *Philebus*. Conceive, for example, that the entity we may call "temperature" has an indefinite range of the more and less hot, of the indefinitely hotter and the indefinitely colder — over which this entity ("temperature") may range and into which it may introduce various pauses of precise qualitative determination. Even before the introduction of such precision, certain loosely defined divisions of the field seem to be related to each other as "hotter" and "colder." Nor are we to limit this new concept to the world of quantity, for it is true also of the medical and ethical orders and we must finally understand that every limiting factor (or *one*) has its own infinite range stretching between two contrary poles as a *place* of operation.[27]

Thus, too, in the *Politicus*[28] there is an order of comparatives closely resembling that of the *Philebus*. The *greater*, an indeterminate, seems to exist only in relation to the *less*, an-

27. It has already been noted (chap. 9, n. 24) that there are those who would identify the "receptacle" of the *Timaeus* with the "unlimited" of the *Philebus*. We need not try to decide that question in this book. On the extent to which the discussion on the limit and unlimited in the *Philebus* relates to the Ideas, see Souilhé, *op. cit.*, p. 69, n. 124.

28. 283d ff.

other indeterminate.[29] If, for example, we take a given speech, that which is longer than this vanishes into the infinite, while that which is less than this comprises another infinite. The two groups of *more* and *less* relate themselves as two poorly defined aggregates. It is only after the introduction of the idea of the mean, or of measure, or of the "right," that the comparatives may now be translated as "too much" and "too little." Thus, not only is the *apt* speech determined but all others can now be measured in terms of their distance of excess and defect from this rightness.

But in all these cases we have a problem somewhat parallel to that which we have seen in the *Timaeus*. I am not suggesting that the principle of the infinite in both the *Philebus* and *Politicus* is the subject of a purely physical description. Nevertheless, the difficulty always remains that the imagination will intervene here too — to interpret that qualities already exist in a confused state and in relation to each other before the work of a limit (or a *one*) begins. Certainly the language used in Hypothesis VII is distinctly the language of the imagination, and we are asked to conceive of the others, or the indefinite, as ὄγκοι, or masses. This is to use terms that, in general, would not have been tolerated in the more careful passages of the *Philebus*. But the hypothesis is describing the world of δόξα and of myth.

What existential status, then, is to be assigned to the indeterminate field of the Platonic "dyad" of the "great and small," the continuum of any two contraries? This is not an easy question; it has been a point of irritation for all the

29. Actually, we should translate μέγα καὶ σμικρόν as a unitary phrase meaning "indefinite quantity."

philosophers who have integrated such a concept into their ontology. The matter, or ὕλη, of Aristotle is certainly a different principle from the ἄπειρον of Plato, but there is the same difficulty in assigning its proper grip on being. Analogously, Aristotle tells us that it is only by a trick of the imagination that his *matter* may be conceived of as *substance* (τόδε τι οὖσα τῷ φαίνεσθαι);[30] it is essentially a relative being — relative, that is, to form. But he is constantly shifting between a view that assigns it a purely relative, even a negative, status and one that assigns it a positive reality. Indeed, we may say that the difficulty of locating matter existentially is at the root of some of the greatest dilemmas in the peripatetic philosophy.

Fortunately it is precisely this question that is examined in the final hypothesis of the dialogue. When it finishes its brief discussion of the dilemma there will no longer be a possibility in any sense that the partial existence of "the other" purely independently of the *one,* or the confused inter-relating of the contraries in Hypothesis VII can be anything but the product of pure "seeming," of a doxa that is opposed to εἶναι.

30. *Metaphysics* 1070a 9. Cf. Hamelin, *Le Système d'Aristote*, p. 265.

12

HYPOTHESIS VIII

The Problems:

The hypothesis is that there is absolutely no principle of unity in an entity. We then reach the climax of the conclusions to be drawn. So much is the one the source of the being of the many, that under this final supposition the many could not be in any way. Not even as indeterminate. Not even as vaguely knowable.

12

To understand the climax now being reached we must come to complete clarity about the differences between Hypotheses III, IV, VII, and VIII. In the pair of III and IV, a *one* is conceived of as existing but as not being its many (or parts); therefore it is separate from the latter. The result for these members or "others" is that of themselves they have an indeterminate being, and where they do *have* specificity it is in a received and participating form. In Hypothesis VII, a *one* is conceived to be withdrawn from contact with its many, but only after the indecisive fashion of δόξα; the result is that the many parts, or others, still have a shadowy though illogical appearance of specificity — they are caught, like the half-withdrawn *one* itself, in a midway region of being and non-being.

Now suppose that we become completely decisive, as we have not been in Hypothesis IV, about the non-existence of oneness in a being. Let us no longer be negative, to the limited degree of saying that it exists as a principle different from and therefore separate from its members. If such were the case it would still be contributing predicability and order to the others, and the latter would be knowable. Furthermore, we are no longer proposing the conditions of δόξα, according to which the *one* is only by premise negated but to some degree remains to give at least confused determination. No, if a *one* really exists in no way, then the results for the "others" also begin to be decisive. We can, therefore, not only repeat the conclusions of Hypothesis IV that all predicability vanishes from them; not only can we fully remove from them even the shadowy appearance of determination and knowability. But it is necessary to go to the limit of denial: the members or parts or "others" in an entity will themselves in no way exist. They, too, like the *one*, will be a pure nothing.

The consequences of this conclusion for our understanding of the unlimited factor are extremely important. For it would still have seemed that, granted all our premises about the non-existence of a *one* or of unity, the indeterminate would still retain some vestige of being as an indeterminate, plus some vestige of knowability — such, at least, as is suggested in the "bastard" knowledge of the *Timaeus*. This is not so.

We are, therefore, again wrong in holding onto an *imaginative* understanding of the relation between a *one* and its many — as though they were two numerically different things, each making its separate contribution to the reality of an entity. Rather, we seem to be invited to understand that the very capacity of the many to make any such contribution at all is given to it by oneness. The imagination must not intervene to becloud the issue. We have already noted how false it is to conceive that the unlimited, apart from the *one*, can exist as a not fully determined chaos. That would be to introduce poetry and myth into metaphysics. But now we advance more deeply into the problem. The unlimited cannot exist even as a pure indeterminate if there be no unities in the world.

13

CONCLUSION

Towards a Summary:

Summary of the most important metaphysical propositions of the *Parmenides*. Participation as the central instrument of Platonism. Six suggestions as to its application. It is a carefully elaborated doctrine; Aristotle is wrong in his contemptuous reference to it as a mere "metaphor."

It is by participation that the dilemma of unity in a many is resolved.

Plato's great achievement in mediating the Parmenidean dichotomy between being and non-being. Various forms under which this dichotomy is resolved by a fusion of being and non-being: the infinite or indeterminate; otherness; relation; the instant.

13

I believe that our analysis of the *Parmenides* leaves us in a much better position to construct a brief but important sketch of a good number of basic positions in Platonic metaphysics. Above all, much light has been thrown on the manner in which Plato views the internal structure of being.

1. *Participation*

I take *participation* as the key word and the key idea that opens many doors and solves many problems for Plato. Rather than being an idle word or an ineffective metaphor, as Aristotle[1] very unjustly calls it, it has now received a scientific elaboration and has become the central instrument of Platonism. It is the constantly recurring theme in our universal logic and has now invaded every order of the real. Its fundamental function is to describe the relationship between the elements of any *one-many* organism and to resolve the problems created by this basic contrariety lying at the heart of all being.

a. There is, of course, no formal discussion of the Idea of the Good and of the separate Ideas in the text of the

1. *Metaphysics* 991a 22.

dialogue, but in it there is a "logic" that can at least suggest the relationship between these two Platonic concepts. I should say that, if we use the *Republic* and the *Parmenides* as two parallel sources of light, we will be in a position to make a judgment on the subject. The Ideas are a "concrete" totality, an organism, whose form and collective unity and total interrelationship are to be found in the indivisible One called the Good. We have no absolute reason to think that the Good was viewed by Plato in the special Neoplatonic sense that is sometimes ascribed to it. That is to say, we need not view it as an entity that has an existence separate from the Ideas, as the transcendental source, according to a relation of priority and posteriority, of the Ideas. If we should apply the concepts of the eight hypotheses, we should already have on our hands a first one-many organism here. Only the Good exists according to an absolute mode of being; the Ideas as perceptible, definable, limited, specifiable entities are the structure, the parts, the members of this One, and as such they exist by the relative mode of *participation*. This is not to say that they are not eternal and unchangeable. For there is no contradiction in allowing the idea of participation to invade the area of the eternal and unchangeable. We will better understand the concept of μέθεξις if we realize that it is an analogous concept that has its place, *mutatis mutandis*, in every field of the real. And we must never commit the fundamental error, as some have done, of identifying the idea of relation and relative being with that of the inferior order of Becoming. For some have decided that there cannot be Ideas of relation in Plato, since by their very essence such Ideas would have to be excluded from the absolute and eternal world of the Forms. It is the word *absolute* that creates the misunderstanding. All is not absolute in every sense in the Ideas, though they are all absolutes and eternal.

At any rate, I would suggest that there is an organic interplay between the Good and the Ideas, which should be described in terms of the logic of the eight hypotheses. The Ideas, if unassociated with the Good, would be a complete field of indeterminacy and multiplicity. But through association they receive all their actual identity, specificity, and limitation. The Good, on the other hand, does not exist in isolation from its members and it is impossible, pure and indivisible that it is, to "know" it except in terms of these members.

b. Analogously, each Idea is structurally composed of a one-many relationship; the one, or pure indivisible in it exists in an absolute fashion; the members or elements or phases of the Idea exist only in a relative and participating sense. It is not possible, strictly speaking, to say that they *are;* they have their being from a *one* that is both different from, yet identical with, its elements.

c. In the order of definition, definition itself is nothing but the purest reflexion, the closest approximation, in the order of human knowledge, to the ontological reality of the Ideas. They habitually receive their most scientific statement in the form of διαίρεσις in the dialogues, a process in which the definition is broken down into a hierarchical multiplicity of factors. Since the human intelligence is of necessity a dividing and a multiplying faculty, it can describe the multiple *elements* or parts of an Idea, but it would be impossible for it to do anything but state the existence of a *one*, a unifying indivisible principle of which the multiple elements are but parts. But such at any rate is the case. And between this definitional one and many we must again conceive the relationship of absolute and relative, being and participation. Unless, indeed, it is utterly paradoxical to assign such real terms to the area of knowledge.

d. Descending to the world of Becoming, we must have the courage to apply the same structural concepts to the internal reality of the sensible. In it there is an absolute that is its *one;* this is, in analogous fashion, a pure indivisible and alone exists in its own right, at least in relation to its elements. There is also a sense in which, as an indivisible, it exists neither in space nor in time and is not subject to change or motion. Analogously, it is not the subject of predication or contrariety and can receive the same description (with the exception noted) that is applied by Plato to the Good, by Parmenides to his One Being, and by Plotinus to the One. But the multiple elements of a sensible, whether these elements be spatial or temporal, only participate in this superior form of being. And together these two factors, the indivisible and the multiple, create the ground for an explanation of such problems of contrariety as are contained in the spatial and temporal continua.

e. If, on the contrary, we look upward from the sensible order to its relationship with the Ideas, then the total sensible, even as a *one,* becomes an entity that must be described totally in terms of participation. Each and all the sensible particulars that fall under one Idea may now be conceived as forming an organism with the latter, receiving being and specificity from that Idea. However, one must locate this relation with extreme care if one is to avoid subjecting the whole Platonic theory to the frequently specious dialectical attack of Aristotle, who is constantly confusing the existential and essential moments of the Ideas. He interprets that the Ideas are not only separate eternal entities (with their own consequent qualities of eternity, immobility, and simplicity) but are also functionally the internal forms of sensibles. This, of course, allows him to discover a long series of hopelessly antinomical qualities in the Ideas, for then they are both one and many, eternal and coming-to-be, and so on in endless fashion. Actually, we must recur here to the principles established in (d) where the sensible is seen to have its own inward and absolute principle of unity and its own principle of multiplicity, neither of which is existentially identical (unless we qualify this word most carefully) with the corresponding principles in the Ideas. Plato, therefore, tells us that the Idea never enters into the sensible to form it as an organism of a One-many! It does enter into the larger organism that constitutes the relationship of the Idea and the collectivity of its particulars. Thus, the sensible should be viewed as an organism within an organism.

f. The same logic can also be applied validly to the problem of the philosophic nature of the number series; and in such a way as to expose the differences between the Aristotelian and Platonic concepts of number. Aristotle would understand that each member of the integer series is an additional composition of separate units and thus would insist over against Plato that there could not possibly be Ideas of numbers. For it would be impossible that such an Idea, so composed, have the indivisibility attachable to the Ideas. But Plato would surely have answered that each number is composed of a one-many, that the *one* alone in it has absolute existence and the so-called elements (of which more presently) only participate in the latter. Thus there is only a single and not a double essence in each integer, and each by the same title is absolutely unique rather than a totality of units all alike (and subject to the severe abstractive unity of such a unit). Actually, it is not possible to say that all numbers are composed of different additive sums of the same, equalized elements.

2. *Participation and Unity*

Very early in this study I suggested that one of the severest problems with which Plato had to deal was the complete dichotomy between being and non-being that had been created by the Parmenidean logic. Let us now consider for a moment how this more sensitively conceived theory of participation has attacked and resolved some of the dilemmas inherent in such a dichotomy.

Participation is a concept that succeeds in locating a world midway between being and non-being. And every metaphysics must locate such a region if it is to have any success in resolving such problems as motion and change in the sensible, and the phenomenon of unity in any complex being in any order. Because Aristotle was particularly interested in the problem of the logical possibility of *becoming*, of various forms of non-being coming into being, he too was forced to find an answer to the Eleatic propositions that would have made such a transition impossible. This he does by his theory of potential being, and much of his metaphysics is an explanation of the qualities of *being and non-being* that are resident in the related Ideas of potency, privation, matter, and genus.

All these notions are attempts to mediate the type of logic that would insist that either a thing is or it is not; and if it already is it cannot come to be, if it is not, again it cannot come to be. If, therefore, there is such a thing as new being in the world, it had in some fashion not to be before its appearance, and must by equal necessity have already been in existence in some fashion. Both these things can be said of potency. But where Aristotle solved dilemmas by his concept of matter and potency, Plato did so by his theory of participation. First of all he thus resolved the ἀπορία of unity.

Unfortunately, it has not been clear that the problem of unity in any composed being involved the same Eleatic structural dilemma. If one is to establish the possibility of real unity or oneness in a complex Idea or sensible or definition or number, it is once again necessary to mediate the dichotomy of Parmenides. For if all the elements of any entity in any order exist on an equal basis so far as their status of being is concerned, if all things in this entity *are* in an "absolute" manner, then they are all in a very real sense absolute units and it is impossible to create anything but the most artificial kind of unity between such members of a Whole. Superficially at least, the unelaborated theory of Ideas seemed to have left itself open to such criticism, and a good deal of the critique of Aristotle is based on such impossibilities *on the level of unity.*

Now the metaphysics of Plato was especially concerned with this ἀπορία of unity, and we must understand how it is resolved by his theory of participation. A brief review of the sketch of the structure of the separate orders of the real as given above will indicate that in each entity in each order there is only *one being*. By his total elimination of non-being, Parmenides had ended by using the concept of One Being on a cosmic scale only. Plato is far more adroit in employing the concept, and in his metaphysics we find it present in every *thing* that is. Everything else in an entity — all its member concepts, or its compositional matter, or its structural parts — exists only by the mode of participation in the "absolute" being or unity of the thing — which dominates, determines, and produces the "parts." These, therefore, exist in a midway status between being and non-being. It is impossible to say, in an over-simplification, that they *are*. But it is equally impossible to describe them in terms of absolute non-being (as in the description of Hypothesis VI). Thus, in the case of the sensible, if I may use an example that will serve a double purpose, there is a double type of midway region that mediates the original dichotomy. Within the organism of the sensible, its parts only participate in the being of its *one*. It is not to be said, over-simply, that they are or are not. And thus we avoid the need of treating them as absolute units from which true unity could never be compounded. For the general dictum of Aristotle would remain true that two things can only become one if they were never two in the first place. But within the larger organism of the Idea-sensibles, the total organism of a sensible, including its absolute principle of being, must be considered as existing according to the mode of participation. It only *shares* in the being of the Idea and it is wrong to consider it a totally new entity which can ever disturb or disperse the original unity of the Idea. There *is* only one absolute in any particular class of entities, and that is the Idea. So far as sensibles are concerned, the whole Platonic description of the midway world of δόξα[2] must take over, as a mediating world between being and non-being. If we now re-assess the nature of δόξα in terms of an explanation based on the participation theory of our dialogue, we will be able to use such a midway kind of thinking everywhere in such a way as everywhere to solve the problem of oneness.

3. *The Infinite*

There is one other principle that has been added to the theory of participation by way of giving it further subtlety and flexibility for the resolution of every difficulty about unity. That is the principle of the infinite or indeterminate. The infinite is again a mediating factor between being and non-being. This time we are looking at something that mediates in the order of determination. If the parts of an entity were absolute non-being, then the result would in each case be a being with the perfect homogeneity and universal sameness of the One Being of Parmenides. If they were determinate and completely specified, we would again be confronted with the impossibility of unity. For we cannot quite completely unify already specified units in such a way as to produce a real, new unity among them. It was therefore necessary to conceive of a principle midway between nothing and determinacy. And this we call the infinite or unlimited. Thus, the very same being that in the order of existence exists only by a participating mode, now (in the order of specification) is determined according to quality and definite quantity by a

2. This word is not used here in the pejorative sense of Hypothesis VII.

new act of participation. It received all its definability and definiteness only from the determining *one*, but of itself is a thorough unlimited. So far as specification goes, it both is and is not.

4. *Otherness*

There are three other modes of being-non-being in the logic of Plato — and therefore three other ways of breaking the Eleatic dichotomy. These are the concept of Otherness, of relation, and of the "instant." They are all types of mediation between being and non-being, and there is some valid sense in which all may be said to be further types of the idea of participation. They "have" their being only in relation to some absolute form of being.

Unity, after all, is but one Platonic problem. Otherness, or difference, is an equally compelling phenomenon that demands an explanation and the development of some kind of theory of "logical possibility." And here again we begin to see in how many subtle ways Plato has modified the original concept of absolute being. If once more we take the example of a sensible, we have seen that it contains an "absolute" principle of being and unity. It also contains an indeterminate set of factors that we call the infinite and that is a combination of being and non-being. But such a sensible *one* is only one *one*, whereas an evidential world fills us with impressions of many other realities. The sensible entity we are considering must, then, in a still further sense, be a compound of both being and non-being. For it both *is* itself and *is not* all the other things that are not itself. To resolve this phenomenon of limitation, it is necessary to realize that each *one* is constructed of an absolute phase of being (by which it is itself according to a mode of full positivity) and a negative phase of non-being that is a negation of identity with anything else. This latter we call Otherness, or difference, and it is immaterial whether we call it relative being or relative non-being. At any rate it only exists by a participation in the positive being of the *one* that it limits or negates. Once again, it cannot possibly be described as absolute non-being, for in that eventuality there would be no such thing as difference and we would be reduced once more to the perfect world-homogeneity of the Eleatics.

5. *Relation*

No world view would be nearly adequate if it restricted itself to an explanation of the phenomenon of limitation and negation in all the *ones* of the world. It would simply have established a logic of difference or of negative relations between things. It would not at all have accounted for the endless series of positive relations that hold between *ones* and that bind the universe together in larger unities of explanation. Therefore, since up to the moment we have limited ourselves to the formulation of a relative type of non-being (which exists only by its relation to the full positivity of a *one* and which explains the problem of negative relationship), we must now turn to the construction of a form of non-being that is not only relative but also positive in its bearing. And thus we shall have to be able to say three things of this new reality: Of itself, it *is not*, for only the positive *ones are* in any absolute sense; but secondly, it *is* in a relative sense (relative to those *ones* it ties together in some bond of explanation); it participates in their being. Thirdly, this relativity is positive in its nature, for the relations in question are positive and no longer merely negative and differentiating. And as a result of all this we are slowly amassing a series of forms of participating being, all of which differ among themselves by virtue of the different problems they are meant to resolve.

6. The "Instant"

Finally, we must not suppose that Plato was uninterested in all the evidence of motion and change that the external world communicates to us. But, as in every previous case, the inevitable ἀπορία of the Eleatic dichotomy between being and non-being intervenes to make the problem difficult in the order of logic, if not in the order of actuality. Plato's explanation is not the explanation of Aristotle, but it encounters the same problem and the same necessity of finding an intermediary reality. There *is* such a thing as change, there *is* an actual moment of transition between A and B. And yet this is a moment that can be said *not to be,* for at this point a one is the full positivity of neither A nor B. It is in process between the two. We will call this mysterious moment the "instant" and will realize that it is a compound of being and non-being. Yet, if we are perfectly to grasp the nature of this entity, we must go further by insisting that it is impossible to predicate either being or non-being of it. For all change is a passage from being to non-being, or the reverse, and the point of passage must be neither of these.

Here we get a fairly accurate picture of the sense in which

Plato is always pairing contraries throughout the dialogue. The different contraries are meant to be a descriptive explanation of the different characteristics of any entity under discussion. Here we are discussing the moment of transition in change, and the sum of the four contraries will serve together as a complete descriptive definition of this moment. There is a sense in which the "instant" is and is not, neither is nor is not, and the sum total of these senses is the limit to which we can go in our explanation of the "instant." This kind of *summarizing* definition of our moment of transition in motion or change can serve as an effective analogy of the nature of all eight hypotheses of the *Parmenides*. If we collect the conclusions of all eight, if we have now seized as one system all the uses of contrary predicates in all the hypotheses, we will have the most accurate possible definition, in Platonic terms, of what a *one* is.

What Therefore Is a one?

If we are to give a metaphysical explanation, in Platonic terms, of the nature and structure of any reality that is truly one, we can give no briefer explanation than a summary of all that has been said of that structure in the second half of the *Parmenides*. Superficially only, this second part has been a bewildering collection of antinomies, an alternation of negations and affirmations of pairs of contraries. We have tried to make sense, step by step, of each such negation and affirmation and have seen that each is a description of some structural element or character in a single entity. A thorough definition of a unity can now only be had by adding the total series of these descriptive propositions so as to form one system of explanation.

For in the first place an entity that is a true *one* contains an indivisible principle of unity. It has not even such divisibility in it as will allow the attachment of any kind of predication to it, and we must therefore negate the possibility of any predicate (or the contrary of the same) being assigned it. It is that principle of full positivity by which the thing is in an absolute fashion itself and nothing else, though even in this affirmation of selfhood we must avoid the appearance of division (Hypothesis I).

This indivisible principle, if it is the dominating and all-important factor in a *one*, is not all there is in it. Indeed, if it were both the beginning and end of our complicated definition, knowledge of it would be impossible, for a pure and absolute unity of any kind cannot be known by the human mind. Actually, any reality is, in some sense or other, a Whole, compounded of oneness and manyness; it is a one-many. More definitely still, and for the reasons we have assigned, it must be described as a combination of a principle of limitation and of unlimitedness. We underscore the truth of all this by saying that it is therefore necessary to ascribe to a *one*, as a Whole, the affirmation, and no longer the mere negation, of a whole series of contrary predicates. This series is itself an evolution of the basic contrariety that such a *one* is both one and many (Hypothesis II).

Through association with the element of pure oneness the infinite or indeterminate emerges as a hierarchical arrangement of specified parts. This is the actual specificity that we see in a sensible, or apprehend as the structure of an Idea in a definition. Only by such association with this definitizing *one* do the parts of any reality become themselves specific and bounded units, all of which now become units or *ones* by this act of participation, and may have affirmed of them the same series of contraries that have already been assigned to the unparticipating but participated principle of unity (Hypothesis III).

Of themselves, however, these parts would be a pure indeterminate without any possibility of specification or limitation. They would, in such a status, receive as predicates neither of any conceivable pair of contraries. And this, in brief, must serve as our description of the factor of the unlimited that is contained as a *one* (Hypothesis IV).

This total structural combination of the limit and unlimited that constitutes any reality in any order of being does not itself exhaust the content of the real, for there are many other such *ones*. The existence of other *ones*, or realities, becomes logically possible by discovering in our entity a principle of non-being that we call otherness and that limits the *one*. To accentuate the nature of the *one* in the face of other realities we declare that it is a combination of the contraries of being and non-being, and once again a whole series of other contraries follow from this basic point (Hypothesis V).

Yet we must for complete clarity understand that this element of manyness in an entity (that is to say, in any organic unity of any kind) is not absolute non-being. Although it is completely derivative so far as its capacity for specification is concerned, we cannot say that it *is not*. I have suggested that the type of being that belongs to it is best expressed by the Platonic theory of participating being, and have defined "participation" as that status of an entity according to which its reality is preserved without adding anything whatsoever to the being which is its source. It is certainly not marked by the type of absolute non-being described in Hypothesis VI.

Finally, the principle of unity in anything is not only the origin of all specification and determined multiplicity in anything; it is also the source of its very being. It is therefore impossible to say, in an absolute sense, that there are *two* forms of true being in a *one*, its principles of indivisibility and of multiplicity. There is only one, and all else derives from that one by participation. In no part of this analysis, of course, are we speaking the language of Neoplatonism. For each entity in every order has its own absolute in which all its elements participate. And apart from such an absolute these elements, these parts, this infinite, would be nothing at all. We would be able to call it neither one nor many, nor could we assign to it any other pairs of contraries (Hypothesis VIII).

This total series of affirmations and rejections of contrariety is, as I interpret, the Platonic definition of a *one*.

BIBLIOGRAPHY

The following works have been of notable help in the writing of this commentary.

ANDERSON, JAMES F. Review of *Les Origines de l'analogie philosophique dans les dialogues de Platon* by PAUL GRENET in "Analogy in Plato," *The Review of Metaphysics*, IV (1950), 111-28.

ARNOU, RENÉ. *Le Désir de Dieu dans la philosophie de Plotin*. Paris: 1921.

BRUMBAUGH, ROBERT S. *Plato's Mathematical Imagination.* Indiana University Publications, Humanities Series, No. 29. Bloomington: 1954.

BURNET, JOHN. *See* PLATO.

CALLAHAN, JOHN FRANCIS. *Four Views of Time in Ancient Philosophy*. Cambridge (Mass.): 1948.

CHEN, CHUNG-HWAN. "Ueber Platons Dialog *Parmenides*." (Unpublished manuscript.)

CHERNISS, HAROLD. *Aristotle's Criticism of Plato and the Academy*. Vol. I. Baltimore: 1944. Only one volume has appeared. I have cited it frequently and refer to it under the brief form "Cherniss, I."

———. *Aristotle's Criticism of Presocratic Philosophy*. Baltimore: 1935.

CHERNISS, HAROLD. "Parmenides and the *Parmenides* of Plato," *American Journal of Philology*, LIII (1932), 122-38.

———. "The Philosophical Economy of the Theory of Ideas," *American Journal of Philology*, LVII (1936), 445-56.

CORNFORD, FRANCIS MACDONALD. "Parmenides' Two Ways," *Classical Quarterly*, XXVII (1933), 97-111.

———. *Plato's Cosmology*. London: 1937.

———. *Plato's Theory of Knowledge*. London: 1935.

———. *Plato and Parmenides*. London: 1939. Cited under the brief form "Cornford, *Parmenides*."

COUSIN, VICTOR. *See* PROCLUS DIADOCHUS.

DAMASCIUS. Ἀπορίαι καὶ λύσεις περὶ τῶν πρώτων ἀρχῶν εἰς τὸν Πλάτωνος Παρμενίδην. Paris: 1889.

DEMOS, RAPHAEL. *The Philosophy of Plato*. New York: 1939.

———. "The One and the Many in Plato," *Philosophical Essays for Alfred North Whitehead*, pp. 41-66. London: 1936.

DE VRIES, E. J. *Spel bij Plato*. Amsterdam: 1949.

DIELS, HERMANN. *Die Fragmente der Vorsokratiker*. 3 vols. Berlin: 1954.

———. *Parmenides, Lehrgedicht*. Berlin: 1897.

DIÈS, AUGUSTE. *La Définition de l'être et la nature des idées dans le Sophiste de Platon*. Paris: 1909.

———. *Autour de Platon*. Paris: 1927.

———. *Platon, Oeuvres Complètes*, VIII, 1, *Parménide*. Paris: 1950.

DODDS, ERIC ROBERTSON. "The *Parmenides* of Plato and the Origin of the Neoplatonic 'One,'" *Classical Quarterly*, XXII (1928), 129-42.

ELSE, G. F. "The Terminology of the Ideas," *Harvard Studies in Classical Philology*, XLVII (1936), 17-55.

FOUILLÉ, ALFRED JULES EMILE. *La Philosophie de Platon.* 4 vols. Paris: 1912.

FREEMAN, KATHLEEN. *Ancilla to the Pre-Socratic Philosophers.* Cambridge (Mass.): 1948.

———. *The Pre-Socratic Philosophers.* Oxford: 1945.

GRENET, PAUL. *Les Origines de l'analogie philosophique dans les dialogues de Platon.* Paris: 1948.

HALÉVY, ELIE. *La Théorie platonicienne des sciences.* Paris: 1896.

HAMELIN, OCTAVE. *Le Système d'Aristote.* Paris: 1920.

HARDIE, WILLIAM FRANCIS ROSS. *A Study in Plato.* Oxford: 1936.

HEGEL, GEORGE WILHELM FRIEDRICH. *Science of Logic.* Translated by W. H. JOHNSON and L. G. STRUTHERS. London: 1929.

JOWETT, BENJAMIN. *The Dialogues of Plato.* 5 vols. Oxford: 1892.

———, and CAMPBELL, LEWIS. *Plato's Republic.* 3 vols. Oxford: 1894.

MILHAUD, GASTON SAMUEL. *Les Philosophes géomètres de la Grèce.* Paris: 1900.

MORE, PAUL ELMER. *Platonism.* Princeton: 1926.

PLATO. *Platonis opera.* Edited by JOHN BURNET. Oxford: 1910. All citations from the *Parmenides* in this commentary are taken from the Burnet text, Vol. II.

PROCLUS DIADOCHUS. *Commentarius in Platonis Timaeum.* Edited by C. E. C. SCHNEIDER. Vratislaviae: 1847.

———. *Commentarius in Parmenidem Platonis,* in *Procli*

Opera Inedita. Edited by VICTOR COUSIN. Paris: 1864. 2nd ed.

RAVAISSON, FÉLIX. *Essai sur la Métaphysique d'Aristote*. Vol. I of 2 vols. Paris: 1837.

RITTER, CONSTANTIN. *The Essence of Plato's Philosophy*, translated by ADAM ALLES. London: 1933.

RIVAUD, ALBERT. *Le Problème du devenir*. Paris: 1906.

ROBIN, LÉON. *La Théorie platonicienne des idées et des nombres d'après Aristote*. Paris: 1908.

———. *Platon*. Paris: 1935.

———. *La Pensée hellénique des origines à l'Epicure*. Paris: 1942.

ROBINSON, RICHARD. *Plato's Earlier Dialectic*. Ithaca, N. Y.: 1941.

RODIER, GEORGES. *Etudes de philosophie grecque*. Paris: 1926.

ROSS, SIR WILLIAM DAVID. *Aristotle's Metaphysics*. 2 vols. Oxford: 1924.

———. *Aristotle's Physics*. Oxford: 1936.

———. *Aristotle*. London: 1949.

RYLE, GILBERT. "Plato's *Parmenides*," *Mind*, XLVIII (1939), 129-51, 302-25.

SCOON, R. "Plato's *Parmenides*," *Mind*, LI (1942), 115-33.

SIMPLICIUS. *In Aristotelis Phys. libros Commentaria*. Edited by H. DIELS. 2 vols. Berlin: 1882-95.

SKEMP, JOSEPH BRIGHT. *The Theory of Motion in Plato's Later Dialogues*. Cambridge: 1942.

SOUILHÉ, JOSEPH. *La Notion platonicienne de l'intermédiaire*. Paris: 1919.

SPEISER, ANDREAS. *Ein Parmenideskommentar*. Leipzig: 1937.

STALLBAUM, GOTTFRIED, ed. *Platonis Parmenides cum quattuor libris prolegomenorum et commentario perpetuo.* Leipzig: 1841.

STENZEL, JULIUS. *Plato's Method of Dialectic.* Translated by D. J. ALLAN. Oxford: 1940.

STEWART, JOHN ALEXANDER. *Plato's Doctrine of Ideas.* Oxford: 1909.

TAYLOR, ALFRED EDWARD. *The* Parmenides *of Plato.* Oxford: 1940. Cited under the brief form "Taylor, *Parmenides.*"

———. *A Commentary on Plato's* Timaeus. Oxford: 1928.

———. *Plato, The Man and His Work.* New York: 1927.

VLASTOS, GREGORY. "The Third Man Argument in the *Parmenides,*" *The Philosophical Review,* LXIII, No. 3 (July, 1954), 319-49.

WAHL, JEAN ANDRÉ. *Etude sur le Parménide de Platon.* Paris: 1926.

WALKER, MERLE G. "The One and the Many in Plato's *Parmenides,*" *Philosophical Review,* XLVII (1938), 488-516.

WEBER, AZARY. *Essai sur la deuxième hypothèse du Parménide.* Paris: 1937.

WERNER, CHARLES. *Aristote et l'idéalisme platonicien.* Paris: 1910.

WUNDT, MAX. *Platons Parmenides.* Stuttgart-Berlin: 1935.